BLACK TEACHER

T0323171

Beryl Gilroy was born in 1924 in British Guiana. She trained as a teacher in Georgetown before teaching in several schools and on a UNICEF food programme. In 1952, Gilroy arrived in Britain to study Child Development at the University of London. For years she was denied teaching positions due to the colour bar, but after finally entering the educational system, she rose to become one of Britain's first black headteachers in 1969, while raising a young family. As well as her memoir *Black Teacher* (1976), Gilroy wrote poetry, essays and fiction, including the prize-winning *Frangipani House* (1986), *Boy-Sandwich* (1989) and *In Praise of Love and Children* (1996), and numerous titles in the pioneering multicultural children's series, *Nippers*. She later gained a PhD in Counselling Psychology and practised at the Tavistock Clinic as well as working at the BBC, the Race Relations Board and the Institute of Education, where she was an Honorary Fellow. Gilroy was described after her death in 2001 as 'one of Britain's most significant post-war Caribbean migrants'.

Further praise for *Black Teacher*:

'A superb but shocking memoir about a brilliant teacher, imaginative, resilient and inspiring.' Jacqueline Wilson

'In a world full of despair, Gilroy is an inspirational breath of fresh air, delivering an empowering tale of courage, resistance, and triumph.' David Lammy

'A landmark book. Warm and wise. Beryl Gilroy has given life lessons we can all learn from.' Jeffrey Boakye

'British literary history could never be complete without Gilroy's lived experience. She was a pioneer in many fields and a wonderful example for all of us to follow.' Alex Wheatle

'Written with a novelist's ear and sense of atmosphere, *Black Teacher* is a vital and unique testament to the tribulations and successes of the Windrush Generation in Britain. Amid the prevailing culture of irrationally racist notions of Afro-Caribbeans – one in which Black women in particular were defined as second-class citizens – Gilroy strode through her career deftly challenging the mindsets of pupils and colleagues alike, while pioneering a path for Black immigrants to the top of British professional life.' Paul Mendez

'Reading *Black Teacher* makes me aware that Gilroy was not only teaching children but also everyone around her how to live respectfully whilst negotiating life in an England riddled with racist ideologies – a particularly impressive and important feat during the 1950s that still remains so now.' Roger Robinson

Beryl Gilroy

Black Teacher

faber

This edition first published in 2021
by Faber & Faber Ltd
The Bindery, 51 Hatton Garden
London EC1N 8HN
This paperback edition published in 2022

First published by Cassell & Company Ltd in 1976
Reprinted by Bogle-L'Ouverture in 1994

Typeset by Faber & Faber Ltd
Printed and bound by CPI Group (UK) Ltd, Croydon, CR0 4YY

Note to reader: This is a reissue of Beryl Gilroy's *Black Teacher*,
which was first published in 1976. The offensive language in these
pages is a reflection of the historical period in which the book
was originally written. It has been retained as it reflects the
author's own experience of discrimination and racism, and
to erase it would be to claim that these
prejudices never existed.

A CIP record for this book
is available from the British Library

ISBN 978-0-571-36698-9

FSC
www.fsc.org
MIX
Paper | Supporting
responsible forestry
FSC® C013604

Printed and bound in the UK on FSC® certified paper in line with our continuing
commitment to ethical business practices, sustainability and the environment.
For further information see faber.co.uk/environmental-policy

2 4 6 8 10 9 7 5 3

TO MY DEAR PAT,
who ceased to live on 5 October 1975

All creatures were his family. His loves were deep and gentle – not rooted in islands of possessions as so many human loves but diffused among people and places, plants and animals, sounds and sentiments, thoughts and feelings.

Acknowledgements

To
my mother for all the past,
my family for their understanding while I
   worked on this book,
my friends who helped with shaping, correcting
   and typing the manuscript,
and the children who made it all possible.

B.G.

Contents

Foreword   xi
Preface   xvii

1 'This school good'   1
2 'I don't mind coloureds'   13
3 'Nobody sent us an invite'   27
4 'She's a real lady'   39
5 'One black teacher'   59
6 'Keep your hands off me'   83
7 'But love 'im I do'   101
8 'I 'ate school'   119
9 'You're a mum, now'   145
10 'She ain't got no spear'   161
11 'Three cheers for group therapy'   177
12 'Black, white, Paki, half-caste?'   209
13 'Someone's happy'   239

Timeline   263
Publications   267

Foreword

Some books always feel fresh and vital, no matter how long ago they were written, and this applies to *Black Teacher* (1976), a memoir full of wit, perceptiveness, humour and compassion. Beryl Gilroy takes us back in time to the fifties and sixties when, as a young woman, she wanted to fulfil her ambition of becoming a primary school teacher in England. Born in 'British Guiana' (now Guyana) in 1924, and raised by her grandparents, Gilroy was initially home-schooled. Regular school attendance began at the age of twelve, followed by teacher training college in the capital, Georgetown, in 1945. She migrated to Britain in 1952 and much of the book covers her early teaching years in London, where she initially struggled to find work due to racism and was forced to take on jobs beneath her level of education.

Anyone who thinks Britain hasn't moved forward in terms of equality and racism needs to read this book. So many citizens of the country Gilroy encountered some seventy years ago had been brainwashed by the centuries-old saturation of racist ideology created in order to justify Britain's role in the transatlantic slave trade and its colonial conquests, with a quarter of the world under British rule at the height of its empire. It's worth remembering that in the early fifties, most of Britain's colonies had yet to gain their independence, either in the Caribbean, Africa, Asia or elsewhere. And here was Gilroy, a black colonial 'subject' trying to make her way in a country whose self-perpetuated myth of its racial superiority was unashamedly thriving, alongside the belief that no matter how lowly people might be ranked in the hierarchy of British society, at least they were white, which elevated them above people of colour.

As a consequence, the level and intensity of blatant racism Gilroy encounters, from small children to adults, is shocking. As a teacher, her students mimic the bigoted nonsense picked up from their parents, but it's easy to forgive them, as she does, because they're too young to think for themselves and their childlike charm wins her over. She understands that her charges have been 'conditioned to consider anything that [isn't] English as downright laughable', and she cleverly challenges their preconceived notions.

The children in her schools are so vividly manifested that it feels like we're in the classroom and playground with them. Voices, often written in vernacular, permeate this memoir, which is so effective in bringing to life the people in Gilroy's environment, especially the voices of the white working classes. Gilroy's phonetic replication of the vernacular is not generally considered wise in fiction these days, as it can make characters sound like caricatures, but it is incredibly effective in the context of this book, and the resurrection of post-war cockney reminds us how much language and culture have changed. Gilroy has a brilliant ear for dialogue; she wants the reader to hear people just as they sound. She has equally finely tuned descriptive abilities. The people she writes about are colourfully and vividly drawn with a few light, bold strokes. It's not surprising that she went on to write novels, because novelistic qualities are at play in her writing, which is teeming with life as we follow the protagonist through the battlefields of fifties and sixties Britain. We are rooting for her, urging her to overcome obstacles and witnessing her personal growth; and we are relieved when she finds love, settles and forges a groundbreaking career.

From start to finish, Gilroy maintains her composure, although she is no pushover. She is a powerfully rooted person, someone whose moral values, sense of humour, innate refinement and dignity rise above the vulgarity of the everyday discrimination hurled at her by people who see only colour and not character. Yes, she is deeply hurt by it, bewildered at first by the behaviour of the uncouth hosts in her adopted country, forced to steel herself against their missiles. A weaker person would crack under the pressure, but Gilroy has arrived in Britain as an adult, already grounded in another culture where the majority of the people are brown and where her right to belong is not questioned. Rather than doubt herself or feel diminished, she regards Britain as 'full of the strangest people'. She discovers that even those with whom she is friendly can stick the knife in, often without realising the gravity of their offensiveness. A co-worker from one of her pre-teaching jobs who is about to move to a smarter part of London tells Gilroy not to visit her because 'I don't want 'em to see me 'obnobbin' with nigs and such. Get it?'

Gilroy says to herself, 'I got it, all right. We'd worked side by side for months, talking and sharing. I couldn't remember when she'd last called me "nig".'

This book serves to remind us how hard it was for post-war immigrants to make their way in Britain when there were so many barriers put before them. However, in case I've misled anyone into thinking this book is a misery memoir, it's not that at all. *Black Teacher* is a fascinating and often funny read, and I relished immersing myself in Gilroy's early life in this country and hearing the Windrush-era story from the perspective of a woman who actually lived through it.

Gilroy had to fight against racial and gender discrimination and expectations; her male counterparts would also have had to deal with physical aggression and violence. This book made me reflect on my own parents. My Nigerian father arrived in Britain in 1949 and had to use his fists against assailants who objected to his presence in this country, which was common-place on the harsh front line of fifties racism. My white English mother, on the other hand, was a recent graduate of teacher training college at the same time that Gilroy was having doors slammed in her face when applying for teaching jobs. My mother literally walked into the first teaching job she applied for. Her issues were about learning how to be a good teacher, not how to find employment in a racist country, nor (once employed as a teacher) how to deal with a racist institution.

While I knew about my father's hardships, I had never previously considered my mother's straightforward and un-hindered entry into her profession – until I read about Gilroy's experiences. Her book really opens our eyes to the realities of fairly recent British history, and might cause us to reflect on the stories within our own families and ancestry, and the things we take for granted, or not. When my mother met and married my father and then went on to have many biracial children, she did, of course, come up against a white supremacy which disapproved of her marriage and her children.

The majority of writers who arrived on these shores in that first wave of post-war migration from the Caribbean were men, the most well known of whom is Samuel Selvon, author of *The*

Foreword

Lonely Londoners (1956). The narratives these authors created about their generation generally featured male protagonists living in an unchallenged patriarchal society. Remember that this was before the second wave of feminism began to question systemic sexism. Gilroy's novel *In Praise of Love and Children* (published in 1996, but actually written in 1959) is the only novel, as far as I know, written by someone of this generation about the female experience of this migration at that time. Readers might be familiar with the names of E. R. Braithwaite, Wilson Harris, George Lamming, Edgar Mittelholzer, V. S. Naipaul, Andrew Salkey and Selvon, but it seems that the sole woman in this cohort, albeit publishing her first adult books somewhat later than the men, has been eclipsed by the light shone on them.

Generations of readers are familiar with *Black Teacher*'s more famous counterpart, the autobiographical novel *To Sir, With Love* (1959) by E. R. Braithwaite, inspired by his time as a schoolteacher in a rough East End school, but Gilroy's memoir has flown under the radar. Yet she was a remarkable pioneer on two counts, as a black female writer (one of the first in this country's history, eventually publishing many books), and as one of Britain's first black headteachers.

Black Teacher has been overlooked, that's the truth of it, barely making the timelines of black British literary history. With its reissue, one hopes that this book will take its rightful place as a hugely important memoir about the fifties and sixties from the rare perspective of a black woman transported to the colonial motherland, leaving behind this brilliant first-person record.

BERNARDINE EVARISTO

November 2020

Preface

Not so long ago a black teacher or a black child was a rarity in Britain. Attitudes to the few blacks then in the country were much the same as they are today but the way people deal with them or react to them has altered. Blacks now assert themselves and demand their rights even if they don't always know exactly what their rights are.

I have lived in England for nearly a quarter of a century. The longer one lives here the more aware one becomes that there is much prejudice but also a great deal of tolerance and a sense of fair play. I resent being called 'a black who has made it' because, every day of his life, a black has to make it with himself. And that's hardest of all.

BERYL GILROY

'This school good'

A September morning in 1969. It was dark, cold and forbiddingly damp. My hands itched despite the cold weather. It was a show of nerves which now plagued me.

'Look,' I said in a bid for sympathy. 'That rash has come back the minute the holidays are over.'

'It'll disappear the moment you get to school,' said my husband. 'As soon as you see the children you'll be as right as rain.'

I had always been a natural teacher. Before I left British Guiana, as it then was, I had made my name as an infants' teacher. My experience of young children was long and deep. Yet here I was, over twenty years later, feeling and acting like a novice. I was afraid to go to school.

Beryl (fourth from right) at teacher training college
in Georgetown, British Guiana, 1943

I was about to start my second term as Headmistress of a North London infants' school of a most unusual kind. Already there were twenty nationalities registered. Later this would rise to forty-four. Multiracial schools had always fascinated me, and in my school there was an interesting mix of social classes.

My experience had shown that children are not born with race and colour prejudice. They absorb it from the adults around them. But since I was the first black Headmistress in the lively borough of Camden, I was bound to encounter bigots of all sorts, the child who would always test me, and teachers who would be inhibited by my colour. I was well conditioned but the memory of the previous term rankled.

What a school! It was a big noisy barn where the children, in a mass of mess and chaos, integrated their day. The process left many of them bored and without purpose and they showed their boredom by throwing the books and toys about, working over each other, charging through the corridors, telling tales about each other and never, never owning up to even the most trivial misdemeanour. I had taught in dozens of schools but never in one in which children so felt the need to tell on their peers.

Lording it over them were teachers who talked endlessly and with passion of their rights. These included the right to treat my office like a thoroughfare, the right to greet me frequently with 'We have decided that you should . . .' and the right to assume as often as it suited them that the school was run by a ghost.

No. I wasn't really looking forward to going back to that place so full of tense, fighting people.

'This school good'

I dressed slowly – not daring to go by public transport. When at last I called a taxi, my mind was made up. I would do what had to be done, say what had to be said and change what had to be changed.

At the school Ade, a little Nigerian boy, met me. He always waited for me since I had smacked him when he hit another boy with his heavy leather shoe. The children had gasped at the sound of leather on flesh and some had covered their eyes as blood trickled down the child's face. Too overcome to speak, his teacher had stood rigid with the violence of the act. I had seized Ade and smacked his hand. It was what his mother would have done had she been there.

'You hit Ade?' a voice had said close behind me. It was Gregory, the self-elected social conscience of the class. Egging him on was Roberta, one of his helpers.

'He can't help it. He's in a home,' said Roberta. 'He's underprivileged. Underprivileged people aren't responsible. My mummy said so.'

'Come along with me, Mr Can't-Help-It,' I had said to Ade. 'You'll find that you will be able to help it from now on.'

I had sat him in my office and given him my family of dolls to play with. Once they had belonged to my own children. They were faded now, but they still had their uses and helped children to act out their feelings and their problems.

'Tell the dolls what you did! They want to hear it from your own mouth.'

He had said nothing but sat with a surly look on his face. Later he muttered, 'I hate white people! Hate them! Hate them!'

'Hate them if you must,' I said, 'but for goodness' sake don't hurt them.'

Now he met me each morning and we planned his day. He was one of those children who were confused by choices; he could not relax in the space around him. All his actions had become compressed into darts and jabs. But now he had learned to trust me.

The school looked bleaker than ever but there was comfort in a cataract of voices – children's voices.

'Miss Gilroy, I like your necklace. Did your husband get it for you?'

'Miss Gilroy, I had my first Communion and some new shoes.'

'Miss Gilroy, I went to Morocco. Did you?'

This explosion of affection, information and trust helped. Despite its imperfections, this was a good place to be. I belonged here. I belonged any place where there were children.

My own day started as it often did with the admissions. I never could have guessed that it would have its own particular sting in its tail.

The corridor was crowded with parents seeking admission for their children. They were expected to attend the school nearest their homes and there was an unusual mixture of nationalities at our school because the area contained a number of embassies, restaurants, colleges and hospitals, in which parents from overseas either trained or worked for periods of a year or more.

I knew that I could admit only twenty five- and six-year-olds and I had opened the door of my office intending to count the waiting children, but immediately an Asian father with two tired-looking, unsuitably clad children rushed in.

He said, accusingly, 'I wait for you since eight o'clock. I must go work.'

4

'This school good'

With some difficulty he told me his address. The children whimpered. I tried to make him realise that he lived in the wrong borough and that I could not take his children.

'This school more near my house,' he insisted. 'This school good.'

The little boy was by now gently dozing and some spittle oozed from his mouth. The father gently wiped the child's mouth with the back of his hand and then wiped his hand on my desk.

He seemed concerned with very little other than his pressing need to dump his children somewhere until he or his wife could collect them.

'Keep them here in one corner,' he said. 'Two 'clock my wife take them.'

But I shook my head and suddenly he swept up the children and hurried from the room.

'They'll be locked in', I thought, 'till Mum comes home.'

Next to arrive was an Englishwoman escorting a Spanish family who hadn't a word of English between them.

The two little girls sat demurely and listened as we talked, the Englishwoman acting as interpreter. The mother was worried about the food. As was the case with many children from overseas, her girls didn't like milk. Would the children starve at school?

I spent a great deal of time reassuring them but they still regarded me with some disbelief as they left. However, the children started school the next day. I was beginning to discover that parents from overseas who had never met a black person in authority required convincing that the black knows how to do the job.

An American mother with an exceptionally precocious son was next. He dragged her through the door and then they both talked of his cleverness, his grades and the various types of therapy the family had experienced.

He told me too of the size of his ego, that he was sensitive about his name and that they were kosher. 'Tell her what kosher means, Mom,' he said.

When his mother showed me his grades instead, he broke into a song, 'Dietary Law-as! Dietary Law-as!'

I took them up to the seven-year class.

'Gee!' Noah blurted out. 'I'm not going to like this class! I'm a hundred years ahead of these kids. Look at them!'

The children were getting ready for their Physical Exercises. Some were in their underclothes and others were arranging socks and shoes in neat piles on the chairs.

'Is this some kind of a nudist colony?' Noah shouted. 'Some kind of a lousy strip-joint? Well, it's not for me. I'm staying in my jeans and my shirt.' He pointed to each item as he spoke.

'It's like this in nearly all the schools in London. Children get undressed and they don't worry about it,' I explained.

In a querulous sing-song voice, Noah stated his opinion of everything in sight.

The children stared at him. Then they started laughing, and after a while Noah joined in.

I went back to the office and admitted Schlomit from Israel, Manase from South Africa, Wayne from Rhodesia, Oliver from Austria, Brigitta from Denmark, Seamus from Ireland, Rama from India, Ester from Germany and Natasha from Russia. Only one of all these children spoke English. When the Russians, a charming, impeccably dressed young journalist and his wife, came in, all the terrible stories one had heard about Russians came flooding back. But their concern for their little daughter was exactly like that of any of the other parents.

She was a beautiful child, clear eyed, composed and relaxed. She didn't play up, fidget, interrupt, shout or show off. Her behaviour seemed based on the certainty of her relationship to her parents, and she accepted her new surroundings and the new situations she met. I commented on how well grown, self-assured and really pretty she was.

'All the children in my country are the same,' said the mother. Both parents spoke excellent English and showed an interest in what was going on in the classroom.

An elegant East African couple was next. She was quite imposing in her traditional dress. Her husband, a delightful man, told us that because the child's name was difficult, the teacher at her previous school had nicknamed her Jenny.

'Her name is a part of her identity,' I said, 'and with your permission we will use it.'

We had quite a task learning to pronounce her name and she seemed relieved when we managed to make the proper sounds. Her name, Nyokilapata, was later shortened to Nyo.

I showed them around, only to meet Noah on the stairs.

'Where did you get that from?' he said. 'The golliwog?' White superiority shone out of his eyes as he pointed to the little girl.

'She's a little girl!' I said. 'Don't you know the difference at your age or are you too mean to notice?'

He shrugged and ran off again.

The sound of a child crying made me hurry back to my room. A man with red hair growing grey at the temples and a disagreeable look on his face awaited me.

'Look at him,' he said, 'all rucked! I wouldn't bring him here 'cept I have to. Where's the uvver 'eadmistress? 'E was used to her. She was doin' all right. Why did they 'ave to change 'er?'

'The Headmistress left here six months ago. I'm the second Headmistress they've had in that time. Where were you and your son?'

'Blacks, blacks. Nothing but blacks everywhere,' he fussed.

'I can't help that,' I said. 'You can't change your hair and I can't change my skin. You can have a transfer for your boy. There are other schools.'

'I don't want no transfer!' he blustered. 'You have one, then we'll all be happy.'

A voice from the end of the corridor called, 'Bill, 'e'll be orright once we're awf.'

'The wife,' he said in a subdued voice.

She came towards me.

'Take no notice of 'im,' she said. 'He gets narked easy.'

'Come on, you,' she said to her son. 'Into the class with you and none of your moanin' and carpin'! You don't want to be like him, do you? A pain in the bloody neck.'

She turned to me. 'By the way, mind if I say something to ya?'

She came very close to me. 'They 'ave an 'at competition every Christmas for muvvers. Mums like me don't stand a chance. Give it a miss this year, aw – go on!'

I had met her kind of mother before. Like their children, they knew they couldn't win in life's race – Life's Hat Competition – so they didn't try. To give her son a different attitude to life I would have to reduce the number of times he'd fail and give him a taste of instant success.

'I didn't even know the competition existed,' I said, 'but give him a few weeks, and he'll settle down.'

A dapper black gentleman in a smart, grey-brown suit came next. He walked with delicate steps and his shoes gleamed like the backs of two beetles. Two children skipped behind him, the girl in a crumpled summer dress and wellington boots, and the little boy with a wary look on his face.

'I'm the First Secretary of ——' He named his embassy.

'I'm sorry,' I said. 'I've admitted all the children I could possibly admit in the five- and six-year group. I'm sorry. I can't help you.'

He frowned at me, his face becoming both dubious and questioning. If anything, it became more so when young Adama, blonde and blue-eyed, reported back from hospital, and little Sally, similarly flaxen, appeared in the doorway to ask me 'out to play'.

The diplomat told me what he knew about English education. 'Children are expected to start school in this country at the age of five years. *You* say you're full up. I will report you to your superiors. I have not seen a black child in this room since I've been here. Only white ones. It's discrimination.'

'Please yourself,' I replied. 'Report me to the Prime Minister if you want to. It won't make a scrap of difference. I haven't got room for your child for one simple reason. The school is full and you were late.'

'My children and I will go to our car and my chauffeur will drive straight to the office of your superiors,' he threatened.

'And the best of British luck to you,' I said.

His aggression came through in the loud voice, the hard unyielding stare, the threatening hand and the expanded chest.

'Sucks!' I said under my breath.

As I walked upstairs I heard angry voices. There was an argument going on between an irascible teacher and a rather pernickety parent.

'I won't have staff quarrelling with parents,' I said. 'Why put their backs up? For teaching their children we get our reward at the end of each month.'

'You're not going to tell us,' said the teacher. 'I worked with A. S. Neill.'

'I don't care if you worked with Plato or Aristotle, Montessori or Bertrand Russell. My name is Beryl and you don't have to work with me. I'm going to run this school my way.'

'We're highly qualified professionals,' said she.

'You can have degrees dripping off you. That has nothing to do with teaching skill,' I replied. 'It comes after a long slog here in the classroom. Why, we've admitted children today from a dozen countries and with them a dozen value systems and attitudes to education. Use your professionalism to reassure the parents. The children have no use for it. What they want is a kind heart and a clear eye when you look at them.'

In my career I had met teachers of all sorts. Those who put on a show each day for their own benefit – who barely skimmed the surface of the children's needs – who wanted to be thought of by colleagues as efficient – who took pride in their ability to 'tell off' the parents – who always blamed the children for not being what they thought children should be. I had met those who must never be challenged or questioned except by children with whom they could identify – the nice children.

For some reason, deep down inside I felt a cold despair and I went off to that haven of peace and enlightenment – the Nursery.

I wasn't there long before a child came to fetch me. There was something familiar about the rotund person in clinging green trousers and worn leather jacket who was waiting to see me.

'You the 'eadmistress? 'Ave you got room in the Nursery?' she asked. 'I got twin little girls of four – we've just moved 'ere. I live in the 'arfway 'ouse not far from 'ere. I want somewhere to leave them while I go to work.'

'Are you unsupported?' I asked.

'Yeah! 'E's gone, my 'usband. 'Aven't seen 'im in years. I've got two kids in 'omes. 'E went back to his country.'

I knew her! Of course I knew her. And it was sad to see that she didn't recognise me. It was Sue. Her voice hadn't changed but time had savaged her. So much time had passed.

Should I reveal myself? I could imagine what she'd say – 'You've done well for yourself, ain't you? Fancy me 'aving to come to you like this! Ain't life narkey?'

Poor Sue! I remembered her vulgarity and her generosity. I remembered, too, the other side of her – her frankness, her carping, and a temper that could flare like a flame-thrower. She had entered my life in the strangest setting – a sort of mail-order sweatshop in London's East End.

2

'I don't mind coloureds'

Prejudice was rare among students, but directly one joined the ranks of the workaday English, life became a fight for survival and dignity.

Just after the war, teachers in other lands were becoming excited by the new techniques, especially those related to child development, that were being pioneered in Britain. I came over to England to study them and all went well until it was time to take off my student's scarf and try to be a teacher. From then on all was frustration. As the months went by, my applications for a teaching post in an infants' school became 'the matter'. Time and again I was told that 'the matter' was being considered. The fact was that, as a Guyanese, I simply could not get a teaching post.

Meanwhile my resources were dwindling and so it was, on a July morning in 1953, I began the job hunt that was to lead me to Sue and her mates.

Things started badly when it was brought to my notice that I was in the wrong queue at the Employment Exchange, but a few minutes later, armed with a card and some addresses in the City, I was on my way. Office number one was quite respectable. It was a modern building, a clean, well-lit glass box. Compared with its neighbours it was like a fresh-faced cherub that had strayed into an unkempt graveyard. With two young men I entered a lift which sped upwards.

The lift stopped abruptly and we stepped out. One man hurried away, but the other lingered. 'Want someone here, miss?' he asked.

'Yes, the manager,' I replied. 'I'm from the Employment Exchange.'

'Oh, ah, you want Personnel. Wait here, I'll get Miss Busby.'

Miss Busby's heels chipped into the floor as if she were trying to carve bits out of it. She wore a green and black floral dress with a close-fitting bodice and flared skirt. So did I. In fact, we wore identical dresses – four guineas from Richard Shops.

'Do you say "snap" or do I?' I said. She eyed me coldly.

'I'm from the Exchange,' I went on, handing her the card.

'Oh dear,' she said dreamily. 'How wasteful of your precious time. The job's gone. Went this morning. I'm sorry.' She closed her file with a click and chipped back the way she had come.

On my way out, the young man in the lift was waiting for me. 'I bet she said the job's gone. Well, that's Mary Busby for you. Just because you're black – nix for you.'

I shrugged. 'I won't go hungry for a while yet.'

The next office was a bus ride away. A sign read 'Multi-Choice Mail Order Stores'. The door stood ajar, an oversized plimsoll propping it open. I knocked.

After a while a slim girl with close-curled hair poked her head around the door. This was Rose, the boss's secretary, I was to learn later. She was like a little lost starlet in that dingy setting, until she opened her mouth and the East End came jumping out.

'What d'ya want?' she gulped.

'Can you say where I could find a Mr Coppett?' I handed her the card.

'I don't mind coloureds'

She slammed the door shut. Suddenly she opened it again and stammered, 'W-Wait here.'

I strained every nerve and listened. There was much whispering and rustling of paper but I didn't have to listen too hard. Quite distinctly I could hear them discussing me. 'Mr Coppett, there's a black girl outside – come about the job.'

'I don't mind coloureds or blacks. They're the same as us,' said another voice.

The door jerked open and the girl with the curly hair said, 'You can come in. Mr Coppett will see you now.'

A tall, slim man sat at a table.

'Are you Mr Coppett?' I asked.

'Are you barmy?' he retorted. 'I'm Mr Hoyt. I'm not 'is nibs.'

From the gloom of the office an elderly man suddenly appeared. He could easily have played the part of a beardless patriarch without make-up.

He spoke through his teeth and twiddled the buttons of his waistcoat as he spoke.

'Sit down,' he said. 'How much will you work for, from nine to five-thirty with half an hour for lunch and two five-minute breaks for tea?'

'A pound a day plus a shilling a day for fares – five guineas,' I replied decisively.

He was silent for an instant. 'Start tomorrow,' Mr Coppett said. 'I like you. You speak your mind.'

The first day was gruelling. There was a backlog of work and I had to win my spurs by clearing the hundreds of cards which littered the table. My job was to file, in numerical order, the thousands of payment cards which came in by post each week.

Late that afternoon Mr Coppett came over to my desk and said, 'You're a college girl, ain't you? I hope you stay here.'

My colleagues were surprised. Evidently it was unusual for the boss to speak to anyone after they had been there for only one day.

Sue was a clever girl with a razor-sharp tongue. Sometimes she looked at life through rose-coloured glasses. When she felt affectionate towards me she would announce, 'Saw another nig-nog today.' When her mood changed she referred to coloured people either as wogs or nig-pigs. That was how she spoke of anybody who wasn't from her road.

She had her ambitions . . .

'A maisonette in Swiss Cottage, that's what I want – a park for me children and no bag-wash clothes for them,' she'd whisper. Her voice would reach a crescendo and her temples pulsate fiercely. She dressed well and would have gone far in school if she had not left at fifteen to do a job. Regularly, meticulously, she filled out her football coupons, wrote 'dead lucky' across the top and posted them. She believed that betting was the only road to a fortune.

I understood her desire for beauty and security.

Then there was Mave who almost invariably came to work wearing her 'berry'. One couldn't help noticing the kind grey-green eyes that peered out of a large speckled face, or her fleshy arms and ample hips. Her body was sensual yet she had an odd fey quality. At times she seemed so far away! Her Terry was very religious and she was devoted to her little boy Bobby.

Liz, on the other hand, was very down to earth. She was the simplest person in that run-down establishment and had the simplest job. After she had addressed the envelopes and checked them against the payment cards, she had to stick on the postage stamps. In front of her was a saucer-sized sponge pad, but Liz never used it. She reminded me of a hungry toad in a flurry of flies when she flipped out her tongue to lick the stamps. Liz often marvelled at my clothes but thought I changed into beads, feathers and bells directly I went back to my digs.

Top of the feminine hierarchy was Hilda, a plump middle-aged woman who was Mr Coppett's right arm. The staff called her 'Needle' because of her cruel tongue and her fondness for that tool of her trade. Although she hardly ever ate in the office she would keep a needle at the ready, just in case she needed to pick her teeth. She was a dedicated woman. She worked with such commitment that she was quite unaware of the beads of sweat that crept out from under her hair and scurried down her temples. Her teeth were stained, crammed together and chipped like ancient brickwork.

Lastly there was tall, thin Mr Michael Hoyt, whom I'd mistaken for Mr Coppett on my first visit. He was to cause me more trouble than the rest of them put together.

Sue talked little about herself. Apart from rushing to 'get Ron 'is chop', or 'best end' for his stew, she never spoke of her husband. She never invited me home. She couldn't. Her in-laws would object to me and she wanted to hide the fact that she lived in one room in someone else's house.

Liz was unmarried. Together with a young nephew, she had lived with her grandmother ever since she returned from wartime evacuation to find herself an orphan. She talked with affection of her nephew and with sorrow of Gran's bad legs. She told me quite casually about the death of her mother when a flying bomb hit their house.

'Me mum was blown to bits and me dad broke his back. 'E died later on in the ambulance. Gran was dead lucky. She only 'ad 'er legs 'urt. They couldn't find any part of me mum 'cept 'er left 'and. Gran knew it was 'er because of 'er wedding ring. Gran never 'ad a penny to bury me dad – every 'arfpenny of their savings blown to kingdom come in the 'ouse.

'We was evacuated, me and Bill. I never thought Mum was goin' to be dead like that. When we was evacuated we went to this school, and a lady looked at me and says to Mum: "I bet she wets her bed."

'Me mum squeezed me 'and and said: "Bet your 'eart away if you like, matey, she don't wet nothin'. Of course she don't." Good old Mum, she was lovely.' She laughed heartily and added: 'After that I never wet me bed again. Though I'd used to wet every night regular as clockwork.'

Her gran was bedridden, Liz said. In the winter arthritis lived in her legs 'as if they was next-door neighbours'.

Hilda was also an open book. But she made depressing reading . . . Dowdy and uncaring about any other activity except the pursuit of profit in trade, she had well and truly missed the marriage bus. The dresses she created were her children and she gave birth to each one in an excited anticipation of gain. By providing her with the tools of her trade and opportunities to sell the finished products to their mutual advantage, Mr Coppett fathered all her children. Any desire for family life and motherhood had long ago been sublimated in the workroom, the office and the dresses she cut. She boomed queries and directions from the most unlikely places. Disappearing down the stairs, she'd announce, 'I'm going to spend.' Moments later her voice would pierce the floorboards like a nail. 'Have you done the green skirt yet? I'll want it ready for packing in a mo'.'

What was left of her attention was given to Mr Coppett, whose mind was three-quarters work-absorbed and the remaining quarter self-absorbed. Besides peering into ledgers, checking numbers, and counting, his only other conscious act was sipping from his bottle of Liqufruta. Hilda sometimes went through the self-imposed task of prinking him, fixing his buttonhole and rearranging the wisps of hair over his balding head, and in a resigned, insensitive way he would let her.

There was never any real let-up to the work in that place. Hilda saw to that. The scrabbled snatches of conversation only served to intensify the pressures we felt. Hilda's eyes darted about like flies, pouncing upon anything she considered 'liberty-taking'. 'Dead liberty!' she'd mutter, as she prowled. 'Dead liberty!' Sometimes boredom hit me like a club, but I was allowed no time to relax. Hilda was always hovering, prodding me on. She'd say, quietly watching me, 'It's funny, ain't it? When someone's not working like a black – someone else is being as lazy as a black. It's funny 'ow these sayin's die 'ard.'

When the decorative, doll-like Rose was away it was the job of any of us girls in the outer office to answer the telephone. One morning, although I was furthest away from it, Mickey (Mr Hoyt) almost compelled me to answer it.

He repeated every word I said and sniggered as he spoke. I was furious.

'Is he married?' I asked Sue.

'Yes,' she replied, 'to an "Eyetie". They adopted 'im, this Italian lot, see. And when 'e grew up 'e married one. She's twice the size of 'im and as greasy as a mutton chop – smells ever so of garlic and such.' Sue pulled a face and covered her nose, as if she expected the smell to materialise and smother her. 'I 'ate it when she comes in the office.'

They all said 'the office' as if they tasted a delicacy every time. It seemed to confer importance, dignity and a sense of pride upon them. It was just one untidy, enormous room arranged in working sections. It was a heaped-up, gloomy place in which lights burned all day whatever the time of year. The only flashes of colour came and went with Hilda and the dresses she carried around for approval. Yet it was 'the office', with a strange identity and a purpose of its own.

As I worked I could reflect upon the differences between the schools I'd visited during my training and the school I'd left behind in British Guiana. School at home was a serious place – a place of struggle and encounter. It wasn't a place where children were expected, except on special occasions, to enjoy themselves. School was work – mostly unpleasant work. Teachers assumed that all children had the ability to learn and the teacher was expected to teach a syllabus approved by the inspectorate. Children were arranged in age-linked stand-ards and were expected to know certain facts, the relevance of which did not always matter. No one thought of individ-ual differences, or of regarding the children as handicapped, or disadvantaged or tired or disturbed. No one thought that the various cultures from which we came had any bearing on what we learned. The way out of the mire of ignorance and poverty rested upon getting some sort of education, and once inside the school both children and teacher found the will to do what was expected of them. Teachers in my country signed their arrival at school the way I now signed my arrival at work.

The only difference was Mickey saying, 'Sign the right time. You blacks wouldn't know the truth even if it bit you.'

Beryl (second row, first right) at teacher training college
in Georgetown, British Guiana, 1945

One day he burst out laughing and put his arm around me.

'You can say what you like,' I spat at him, 'but don't you ever, ever put your hands on me again.'

'Oh, don't get your knickers in a knot!' Mickey grumbled, trying to imply that it had all been a joke. 'Bwana is doing you a favour.'

I was sure he was trying to diminish me in my own mind, and to lodge within me a little seed of doubt.

I often asked myself questions about my people. Were we, as a race, unreliable, thievish, dirty and lazy? After all, I didn't know *everyone* outside my family, outside my village. And what about the one-bath-a-week whites? What of those who washed kids with spit? Were we worse than them?

Sue tried to help me with Mickey. Whenever he started to get at me she would try to take the wind out of his sails. 'Not

21

today, Mickey, for Christ's sake,' she'd say. 'Put a sock in it! We've heard it all before.'

But I still awaited my chance to get even with Mr Hoyt and, strangely enough, it came through the telephone. I answered it one day and a voice said something about Philomena.

'It's Mickey's faggot!' Sue whispered over her cup. I looked at him hooped over his desk. At last – at last he was delivered into my hands. I remembered his most recent barb – 'I know *your* sort of black, wearing a bit of toffee-nose civilisation. It's all on the top. I can scrape it off like paint.'

'Shall I tell her about us, Mick?' I said loudly, spilling it over into the receiver. There was the slightest soupçon of sin in my voice. 'Don't you think she should know about us? After all, we do have lovely times together, don't we?'

Mickey hurtled headlong over some boxes and clutched at the telephone. At the end of the shouting match which followed, he put down the phone, gave us all one terrible glare and stomped out of the room.

'Don't like being paid back, does 'e?' said Liz.

Mickey went out several times that afternoon and I began to blame myself and said so.

'Wouldn't bat an eyelid over 'im,' Sue consoled me. 'After all, he done it in Africa – went for their maid, 'e did. Told me hisself. Said she only had beads round her middle and bosoms like chunks of burnt meat.'

And then, in a matter of moments, there seemed to be a change in both mood and front.

'*You* should have dealt with Mickey,' Mave said severely. 'You shouldn't have brought in his wife.'

It seemed to me like the last straw. 'Mickey attacks every

black person through me,' I snapped. 'He condemns and criticises a whole race through me. What do I care about him and his family? I'm fighting dirty, and I'm glad of it. I've learned it all in this mouldy office and I've had good teachers.'

I walked to the bus stop alone that afternoon. The girls, looking worried and bewildered, followed in a group behind me. I couldn't help hearing Sue demurring in a whine, 'After all, I s'pose you can't blame 'im reelly. Them natives *are* disgustin'.'

Early at work next day, I stood waiting in the street. It had been swept clean but nothing could ever sweep away the smell of dank poverty. Frost had settled slightly on the small circle of glass inserted into the neighbouring door, making it appear like a single, sorrowing, tear-stained eye.

Hilda bustled up and opened our door. 'Nippy, ain't it?' she said. 'Proper brass monkeys!' I nodded my agreement and we started up the old iron staircase.

Mave came in as I took my coat off. 'You're bright and early,' she said, without looking at me.

I ignored her and began powdering my nose. Liz had noticed my powder dozens of times, but this morning, when she arrived, she commented nervously, 'Cor! Ain't your powder brown. That's nutty-brown, ain't it?'

'Some people', I told her severely, 'call it nigger-brown.'

Sue entered the room quietly. 'Mornin' all,' she piped, but I showed no enthusiasm for her either.

'Over 'ere,' she called to Liz and Mave. 'Come over 'ere a minute.' They whispered animatedly for a few seconds, and then came over to me.

'From now on', Sue said, 'we're going to back you up. We

'aven't been 'elpin' you, see. But from now on it's goin' to be different.'

'I shouldn't need help,' I said. 'Common courtesy should be enough. Help Mickey. I reckon he's the sick one. I reckon he needs a doctor.'

Mickey shuffled in, as if on cue. He looked indeed as if he needed a doctor. The spark had gone from him. He saucered his tea without a word and the wrigglings within his suit were only tokens of the old ones. He sat like a man fearing the worst and I quietly rejoiced at his misery. I hoped that his wife and her family had, as Sue said they were capable of doing, attacked him when he went home.

Whatever he feared, it all came true soon after the lunch-break, when we heard strident voices in the workroom. Hilda was being out-shouted. It was a feat in itself. The footsteps and the shouting drew nearer and racing after Hilda came a tall, well-built, muscular woman. The girls gasped.

'Mickey's faggot,' whispered Sue.

Everything about her appeared to have been twisted or spannered into place. Her hair was screwed into a tight knot, her face into a permanent scowl. She seemed to have been bolted into her clothes. Her voice was the only unrestricted thing about her. It flowed ahead of her, full and free – rush, gush and crescendo. She took one look at Mickey and he covered his eyes with his hands like a child overcome by a horror movie.

'The dirty peeg!' the woman shouted. 'I weel keel heem.'

'Now, pull yourself together, Phil,' Hilda begged. 'Don't do your nut in the office. We're all friendly in 'ere, ain't we, girls? Nothin's goin' on 'ere.'

Philomena's eyes started probing, lingering on each of us

24

in turn, as she tried to decide which one was the most likely subject for Mickey's extra-marital attention.

'Look,' I said, 'I answered the phone.'

'You answered the phone?' she asked, her voice vibrant in its disbelief.

'Now, Beryl's a respectable girl,' Hilda said soothingly.

But somehow these very words had worsened things for Mickey Hoyt. She walked over to him, her eyes narrowing.

'I keel you! I keel you!' she screamed.

Mickey looked up with a wan kind of desperation. 'Oh go on – push off. Don't make a fool of yourself in front of people.'

They were brave but stupid words. She moved with amazing speed and applied her bulk to his thin frame. She grabbed him by the neck and shook him. She shook him until the money chinked out of his pockets and spilled on the floor.

'Phil! Phil!' Hilda yelled. 'Now you get out of 'ere before you do damage.'

And somehow she got her through the door.

'Bloody fool of a woman!' muttered Mickey, and then he sank on his knees and started picking up pennies.

After a while I said to him, 'Africa is miles away, Mickey,' and borrowing Hilda's pet phrase, I added, 'Why not speak as you find?'

He resisted me for a moment and then impulsively offered his hand.

'Shake,' he said. 'This is an apology and it's British. I went too far. Yes, that's what I did. I simply went too far.'

As he spoke he appeared to be performing some major surgery inside himself. Equally I felt all the hatred of him going out of my heart.

It was the end of any trouble between us. But it was also a moment of acute embarrassment. Hilda, however, spread her own kind of balm in her own obsessive way.

She came in with satins of many colours draped all around her, her lips moving as if she were talking to them in a most intimate way.

'Coo, look!' she said. 'Ain't they lovely? Ain't they smashin'? I really 'ave got some good clobber in the pipeline.' She came up to me. ''Ere, feel the quality.' She attempted a chipped, cigarette-stained smile. 'And now let's press on, eh? Let's get the show on the road.'

Hilda and her way with dresses never failed to fascinate me. She'd place them in a box with all the tenderness of a mother for a dead child but once they were on their way they were out of mind. She'd work hard and tenderly at the next lot, musing over colours, treasuring new fabrics. It seemed to be a perpetual process of creation and re-creation.

'How can she be the way she is?' I asked Sue. 'She seems happy enough.'

'Don't know no better,' Sue replied. 'Mind you, she ain't short of a few bob. 'Er cat is what she lives for, really. Gives it an 'ole 'alf pound of butter to lick. One day they'll open 'er door and find 'er dead.'

3

'Nobody sent us an invite'

I began to despair of ever getting a teaching post. There had been a time when I'd arrive back at my digs each night and expect my wise and sympathetic landlady to hand me a letter from the Divisional Office saying I'd been fixed up at last.

But as the months went by I didn't really expect a letter any more. I cast around in my mind for some other way to get into teaching and it seemed to me that a job in a church school was the answer. I had always been a good Anglican – an ex-Sunday school teacher – and I regularly attended a church in South London. I knew they wanted an infants' teacher in their local school and so I applied.

I wasn't even called for an interview. The priest put a fatherly hand on my shoulder and told me, 'You see, it's difficult, my dear. I know you're a good person and Christian, and I'm sure you're a gifted teacher, but don't let's forget that the children are at an emotional age. And then there's the parents. I'm afraid they just wouldn't accept you.'

He said this with the implication that I should understand. Well, I didn't. There was no one in the school doing anything I couldn't do. And the parents, who were they? Once-a-week Christians, to be sure.

I was becoming short of cash for Christmas, and one lunch-time I saw a card in a window littered with junk, advertising clerical work. Thinking that a change from Mr Coppett and

Co. was about due, I pushed the door open. A bell muted with dust and age pinged gently. No one stirred. I peeped into the deep gloom. It was then I noticed a man sitting at a table eating a ham roll. Fiercely he bit off a large mouthful and, as he chewed, a slither of ham danced on his chin like a worm on a line. I stood waiting and after what seemed like hours, he turned his head ever so slightly. 'Hello,' I said. 'Came about the job.'

'Can't you read the card? It says no blacks wanted.'

I went to have another look at the card.

'It doesn't,' I said.

'Well, it bloody well ought to. I don't expect blacks to come 'ere pestering me when I'm 'aving my grub. You clear off – you hear me? Clear off.'

That was my only effort to earn more money for Christmas.

The festival brought a flurry of activity to our office.

'Cor,' said Hilda, 'I can't 'ave all this cutting done wiv two 'ands.' And fussed some more.

On Christmas Eve Mave, who always preferred last-minute shopping, slipped away to the market and came panting up the stairs, carrying a large Christmas tree.

'Hi, hi!' said Hilda. 'What we got 'ere then? Ooh, ain't it lovely? Lovely and spiky. Now why don't we 'ave a tree like this and do ourselves a party?'

Mave looked up at her and said, explosively for her, 'Here, take this one. I'll get another on the way home.'

At the news of the tree we all became children again. Excitement grew from a spark to a flame. Hilda worked like the proverbial black, decorating, prinking, handing, matching, chopping and changing the tree until it stood resplendent.

We went back to our desks and worked until four that afternoon. Then Hilda suddenly cried, 'Shut shop, girls! Off to the workroom with you – drinks are on me.'

We followed her into the room. The large table on which she cut her dresses was beautifully set out with gleaming glasses and bottles of cider and sherry. She handed round the glasses brimful of drink – sherry for some and cider for others. Mave gulped her sherry and left soon after. That was more like Mave.

Mr Coppett still sat at his desk, pieces of paper crepitating at his touch, his back ageing and hunched. He sat there intent and involved – silently sabotaging, we thought, any enjoyment of the party. He seemed neglected, solitary and sad. Impulsively I took an undersized cone-shaped hat and placed it on his head.

'We want to toast you, Mr Coppett,' I said. He smiled briefly, as if I had made the most natural remark in the world, stood quite erect and waited.

'To Mr Coppett,' I said.

'To Mr Coppett,' reiterated all the others. He bowed, skimmed his sherry with his lips, removed the party hat as if it symbolised something rare and beautiful, and then with an expansive gesture settled down to his work again. He took no further interest in us and later disappeared like an apparition at dawn.

There was one further toast to come. As if inspired by my tribute to Mr Coppett, Sue stuck her face in Hilda's and cried in her vibrant, generous way, 'Three cheers for the old girl wot puts 'erself out – for everyone!'

Hilda blushed a deep crimson, evidently touched by this quite unprecedented and unsolicited testimonial of regard.

Or she might have been suffering a pang of guilt at the sheer, shaming untruth of it.

Anyway, she was momentarily overcome and left us briefly, murmuring, 'I'm goin' to . . .'

We filled in the dread word for her.

Mickey elected himself Master of Ceremonies. He fished out a bottle of gin and drank it neat between swigs of sherry.

'I *like* Christmas,' I said, as I topped the glasses with the last of the sherry, and somehow, instead of leaving soon, we lingered.

'So do I,' replied Hilda. 'Everyone does. I don't know 'ow they come to mix a nice time like Christmas with all them animals and such – cows, sheep, donkeys and all that lot.'

She made a wry face. 'Fancy 'avin' that poor baby in all that cow dung. All them flies and smells.'

'There weren't any dung there,' chimed in Liz. 'Me gran said God 'elped them cows to 'old it. 'Ave you ever seen any of it in the pictures about Christmas?'

I found this extremely amusing.

Just to show they really accepted me they gave me first go in what they called 'the carsey', saying: 'Go on, Beryl, you can 'ave first go.'

When I came out, Sue eyed me with a look of prurient curiosity.

'Not bein' rude,' she said, 'just bein' inquisitive. What do natives do when they . . .'

'Go to bed?' I asked.

'You know,' she said, self-consciously gesturing, 'your monthlies.'

'You mean when we menstruate?' I asked.

She nodded.

'Well, Sue,' I replied with mock seriousness, 'we swim! We jump into the nearest river and swim and swim for miles. Some of us swim for three days and some for four, but that's what we do.'

I put on my coat and slipped out. The cold gripped me fiercely as I hurried to the bus stop, past windows that now seemed tawdry with their flimsy paper chains and cotton-wool snow. The shadow thrown by a street lamp showed that I still wore my party hat, an untasselled fez. I flung it into the gutter. It was then that I saw a man watching me from across the street.

'Hullo,' he said. 'How are you, my beautiful Caribbee?'

I didn't know what to make of him with his spivvy clothes and heavily greased hair parted in the middle. I didn't wait for more. I ran back to the office. Panting, I ran up the stairs and into instant comfort, directly they all knew what had happened. I'd been 'chased'. This had a weird significance for them. It seemed we were sisters under the skin, all right, when it came to the threat of rape.

There was much talk about dirty old men.

'Anyway,' Hilda said at last, 'it's an ill wind, ain't it? You see, we forgot to give you your present. Fancy that, now. We got somethink special and we forgot to give it to you. Just the thing to cheer you up now you been chased.'

I opened the parcel. It contained a tiny bottle of perfume and a beautiful scarf of brilliant red.

'D'you like that scarf?' Liz asked, the deep concern in her voice ringing like a lump of sugar in an empty teacup. 'I got you that. Changed it three times, I did – just like traffic lights. First I got green, then orange, then I got red.'

I spluttered into my glass, and then I laughed. How could one cap that, especially when she was so obviously thrilled that the gift pleased me.

I got out my own small gifts and handed them around. I hadn't forgotten them. It was just that I was mortally afraid of being the first to give . . .

After the holidays most people talked of the office party with pleasure but soon we settled down to the work – some with resignation and others with hope. I hoped that the New Year would see me teaching but then I dared not hope too hard.

Sue had a black eye which advertised her bickering with Ron.

Mave's attitude worried us. Something seemed to have died within her over the holidays. She seldom spoke and her eyes often looked red and swollen. She simply shrugged if we pressed her with questions. And then, one afternoon, she burst into uncontrollable sobbing. In an instant Liz pounced upon her, cuddling and rocking her.

'It's my Terry,' Mave moaned. 'Took my little boy, he did – and made off with him to Australia, last week. Sneaked him away. I never expected him to take my boy.' She started to cry again. 'He went off with Sylvia, the deaconess at the church.'

'Never did like that louse,' Sue snapped. 'God this, God that. And now taking your Bobby! Ain't men crap? I mean, 'e ought to 'ave left you your nipper.

'All men's a load-a crap, even my Ron,' she added, stroking her eye.

'Men ain't all crap!' Liz said peevishly. 'I'm gettin' engaged to Bill Brazier. Me gran got 'im for me.'

Beryl in Trafalgar Square, London, 1954

'Your gran never leaves 'er blinkin' bed,' Sue objected. 'Sits in it all day like in 'er ivory tower. How come she done that?'

'They come round our 'ouse – the Braziers – to see my gran. 'Is mum is my gran's friend, see. They brought round Christmas greetings. Then Gran said to Bill Brazier, "What, you thirty-three and not married! Why don't you 'ave our Liz? Don't you fancy 'er?"

'"Gran!" I shouted at 'er. "I don't love no one. I don't love Bill."

'"Love's not everythink," my gran said. "If a man marries you, looks after you, and gives you money – you don't 'ave to 'ave the wind up."'

'I know Bill Brazier,' said Sue. 'As soppy as bread and milk. You ain't going to marry 'im?'

'Yes, I am. Next Easter, I am. And I'm goin' to buy me dress next week,' Liz replied.

Even Mave smiled through her tears and gently remonstrated, 'But Easter is months away.'

'I know,' Liz replied. 'But I'm goin' to buy me dress next week.'

And so the weeks passed. Liz's wedding was postponed. Mickey left to manage his father-in-law's new restaurant and Dai, a blunt Welshman, filled Mickey's post.

'How did a lady like you come to work here?' he asked me, rattling his consonants like noonday thunder. 'Among these brats that have hardly learned how to scribble?'

He left us, too, and the same week they found Mave dead in her flat. She had swallowed two hundred aspirins and a bottle of gin. She left a suicide note – quiet and polite and full of quotations from the Bible.

At first the girls seemed bewildered by her death.

''Ow could she do such a thing?' sighed Sue. ''Ow come she didn't tell us she was so worried – so worried as all that?'

'We must send a reaf to the parlour when the police 'ave been,' said Hilda.

Sue nodded and tears welled up in her eyes. 'When I think of that louse, Bible in one 'and, shaggin' 'isself silly with that deaconess in Australia, I could spit,' she said.

''Oo'll take the reaf?' asked Hilda. 'I can't – I'm Jewish.

'We'll have to spend a bob or two,' she went on. 'Twenty-five bob's not too much for poor old Mave. Let's get 'er an 'eart-shaped one. But 'oo'll take it?' she appealed again, now in tones of mingled desperation and irritation.

'I will,' I said, since it was obvious there was going to be a lack of volunteers. 'Just tell me where to go.'

There was a general air of relief now that I'd volunteered. That was that and it was out of the way. Now life could pick up again and go on.

They puzzled me. 'What's wrong with you all?' I asked. 'Wasn't Mave your friend? Can't you talk of her with love and affection now she's dead?'

I felt deeply sorry for Mave. With Terry gone, with her child gone, there was no real point to life any more. At least that was how it must have seemed to her when she reached for the aspirin bottle.

The girls knew all this, but somehow death itself had robbed her of any sort of right to their affection. Talk of death seemed the great taboo. Now she was gone and they wanted her to drop out of mind, rather as if she'd opted for a long holiday.

Besides paying all the funeral expenses, as we learned later, Mr Coppett gave me as much time off as I needed to take the wreath. He offered to drive me there but I declined. I wanted to walk. I went on past the derelict houses, bomb sites, and factories, and the wreath in the box became more burdensome the further I walked.

As I passed a paper factory a row of men wearing cloth caps stood outside and began smiling and shouting at me. I suppose I must have been a very unusual sight for those parts. I couldn't imagine what they were saying, it all sounded gibberish to me. Whatever it was, they found it extremely funny because even a toothless old gentleman with a white beard sprouting on his face laughed heartily.

At last I reached the funeral parlour and went in. I was astonished to find that Mave was to be buried at one-thirty that day. So why hadn't the others come? It was during their lunch hour. A few people stood around – about ten in all. At intervals a low moan, a sob or a sigh filled the little room.

I could see the coffin, a focal point in the room. It was covered with flowers and encircled by the group. The inscription gave her age – twenty-five years.

A murmur, a moan, the odd tear. This seemed all Mave had earned in her short lifetime. I thought how little space one needed when one was dead. She'd been a solitary girl but never boxed in. I laid the wreath on the coffin; it was such a lonely place to be.

'Good-bye, Mave,' I said. 'Goodbye from all of us,' and I went back the way I'd come.

The men were still standing there – still grinning and shouting nonsense. I walked over to them and said, 'Are you Englishmen? If you are, you're a peculiar kind. Englishmen don't stare and shout at women. I've never known them to. Who are you? Do you really know?'

Their surprise gave way to embarrassment. The toothless old man doffed his cap and walked away. I didn't look back at the others.

When I got back to the office I asked, 'Didn't any of you know that the funeral was today?'

'Did 'ear somethink like that, yes,' Sue said.

'Well, why didn't you all go there?' I asked. 'There were only about ten people in the parlour at the most. After all, she worked with us day after day.'

'But nobody sent us an invite, Beryl,' Sue said, a conciliatory note in her voice.

I was aghast. 'An invite? Do you mean to say you expect an invitation to a funeral? Surely, you just go to a funeral. Where I come from you do. You go because you care.'

'Well, over 'ere, mate, someone invites you,' Sue said, as if giving a lesson. 'They comes and tells you where it is and when it is.'

We were all on edge, snapping at each other's tails rather like overcrowded pigs. But the overcrowding, if that's what it was – and I'd never noticed it before – was coming to an end. Mave's death somehow set the pattern for break-up.

Sue's escape was in strict contrast to Mave's tragic exit. Luck had looked her way at last. She'd had a good win on the Pools and announced her departure for Swiss Cottage and the good life.

And her attitudes – her attitude to me in particular – changed accordingly.

'Now look, Beryl,' she warned, putting a farewell hand on my shoulder, 'we been mates, but I don't want you to come visitin' me, see? Wouldn't do,' she explained, 'not with the sort of people where I'm goin'. I don't want 'em to see me 'obnobbin' with nigs and such. Get it?'

I got it, all right. We'd worked side by side for months, talking and sharing. I couldn't remember when she'd last called me 'nig'. But now it seemed that was all wiped out – rather in the manner that Mave had been disposed of.

It was a strange country, full of the strangest people. It was as if no one ever made any lasting friendships. On impulse, I handed in my notice. Hilda shrugged and Mr Coppett's expression on hearing the news was as enigmatic as when he'd heard of Mickey's advancement to the rank of restaurateur and Sue's bit of luck on the Pools.

But there was a modest token of appreciation in my wage packet at the end of my final week. One guinea, to be exact, from Mr Coppett.

We shook hands on the day I left – I can still feel his clammy handshake and smell his misty breath so impregnated with Liqufruta.

As I walked down the staircase for the last time I heard, like echoes in my mind, the voices of Sue, Mave and Liz, as I'd heard them discussing me behind the doors on the day when I'd waited outside before that little doll Rose ushered me into a world beyond all previous imagining. I noticed that the plimsoll still held the door ajar.

Well, now I was leaving it all, and for a moment the untidy piles of clothes, boxes, string and paper stirred in me a faint feeling of nostalgia.

Hilda waved me goodbye, but it was Liz – now last but one of the old brigade – who had the final word.

This was wistful, too. 'Now, don't forget my wedding, love, whatever you do, will you? Ta-ta, Beryl – all the best.'

4

'She's a real lady'

There was at least an improvement in my next job, even if I couldn't claim any real advancement in status. Two days after saying goodbye to Coppett and Co. I sat over coffee with Sarah Denner, a student counsellor, lamenting my failure to get employment as a teacher and chuckling through my experiences as a filing clerk.

Sarah was a good friend to students from the British Empire, as it then was. She listened and sympathised. At last I said, 'Uh-uh! No more office work for me! I'd sooner be a maid to any rheumaticky old crock.'

'Fine,' said Sarah. 'You've got a job. I'm looking for a student willing to work as a kind of maid for a month or so. It's for Lady Anne. You've met her, surely. All students meet her sooner or later. She's one of those unforgettable people. Committed flesh, blood and bones to Empire building.'

I remembered her well. She had entertained us at a party in the university. We wore cardboard buttons with our names and our countries of origin and she walked round greeting everyone and reading off our names in a loud voice.

Her ancestors, it was said, had given years of dedicated service to sovereign and Empire, and by offering brief spells of culture-oriented employment to students from different countries she brought them as close as she dared to people of genuine English bloodstock. Presumably her intention was partly to chasten and partly to instil. Into her chosen 'children' she could instil whatever she chose. 'Englishness' was a favourite word. 'Leadership' was another.

Beryl as a student at the University of London being presented to
Edwina Mountbatten, Countess Mountbatten of Burma, 1952

She always spoke in the top register and unless one listened very carefully, her words reached the ears as strangely garbled sound. She had talked to us about enlightened self-interest and warned against uninformed clamour for independence. Then she wished us a profitable stay in this 'old and wonderful country', and invited us to contact her office without fear if ever we needed advice.

She proved herself a skilful and demoralising speaker whenever the students tried to embarrass her. The Open Air Theatre was that evening performing *Romeo and Juliet* in Regent's Park and she hoped some of us would attend.

'We are Africans,' protested Rabat Mahmoud. 'What good is Shakespeare to us? We don't want Shakespeare and we don't want colonisation.'

Extending her vowels like elastic, Lady Anne had replied, 'Have you now got a Shakespeare of your own, young man, or is there still a literary void in your country? What are you studying?'

'Law, my lady,' Rabat replied.

'Then you are in no position to pronounce upon literature.'

I called at her office the next day, to discuss the terms of my employment.

'Are you the one who visited schools to tell of your native land?'

'No, my lady,' I answered.

'Then you must be the one who addressed the ladies of Poplar last autumn.'

'No, Lady Anne. I am the one who would like to be your maid. I am from Miss Denner.'

'Ah, yes,' she said. 'The light of day at last. You'll do perfectly well. Come to my house tomorrow at nine. You know Bayswater, do you not?'

'Yes, my lady – I live in Highgate.'

'Ah, Highgate – it is not too difficult a journey. Well, then, goodbye. I will see you tomorrow at nine.'

As I rose, her keen, clear, blue eyes slowly explored me – resting here and there like the beam of a torch and capturing every detail of dress and appearance.

'You stand very well. I suppose you come from a long line of carriers.'

'Not exactly, my lady,' I replied. 'I come from a long line of teachers and farmers.'

Lady Anne, who was about sixty, wore a heavy tweed skirt, sensible shoes and a practical felt hat, but the next morning, in the warm, pastel-coloured elegance of her drawing-room, yellow-tinted with early spring sunshine, she seemed years younger. We talked for a while and then she said, 'Now to work! The uniform first of all.'

My uniform consisted of a blue linen dress and white cap and apron. It amused me seeing myself dressed as a maid, but it was an experience, and experience, I'd been told, meant growth. She told me, in a manner which suggested dicing crisp vegetables, what my duties were.

'I breakfast in my room,' she said. 'A cup of tea and half a grapefruit. You must answer the phone by saying that it is my residence. I lunch at home on impulse. You will tidy up generally – after I leave each morning. I'll come and talk to you from time to time and give you the necessary instructions. A man from the agency calls to clean on Thursdays.'

I soon discovered the immense range of her intellect and was fascinated by her vast knowledge of everything English. She made me feel a little ashamed of my scant knowledge of my Guyanese heritage. She had an inner quality – a dignity and quiet authority which permeated her every act. True, her clothes were dated and her face had succumbed to the ravaging years, but her whole style was outside anything I had previously experienced. I concluded that this was what 'class' meant: a certain assurance of self, of position and of the direction which attitude and energy must take.

Exhilaration at being surrounded by her beautiful possessions came over me daily. The china was exquisite and, as I enjoyed a drink of cold water from one of her delicious antique teacups, I felt warm and friendly inside and a little guilty – rather like the native who sipped forbidden whisky. I was astounded by the craftsmanship of the paintings and etchings that graced the rooms. The feel of perfect English furniture and the glorious softness of her rugs enraptured me. I felt myself gaining and growing after only a few days in those surroundings. I had always imagined a lady to be totally aware of social distance – to be snobbish and patronising. Lady Anne was none of these things. She behaved naturally, gracefully and with absolute ease of manner.

I assumed that to be so knowledgeable she must have toiled for years at university and expected her to have academic degrees as long as a clothes-line after her name. What an enigma she became when I discovered that all my assumptions about her education were false!

'My governess, bless her, laid siege to my mind,' Lady Anne said, smiling amicably. 'She was an intense and vigorous woman, genteel at all times, devout on Sundays and uncompromising for the rest of the week.'

I thought of my own schooldays and the hours we spent chanting spellings, tables and facts of all sorts in sleepy chorus. I called to mind the teacher we nicknamed 'Prompt Obedience' with the clear, sharp perception of children. Each day after lunch, when the noonday heat held 'Prompt Obedience' in thrall, she snatched forty winks. Her cloud-coloured, cotton-wool hair emphasised the proportions of her drooping head in a way which filled me with terror. However sound her sleep, the long tamarind rod she clasped in one hand could awake immediately into terrible life.

We had no library in my village school before I was twelve,

but as I had read all the popular children's classics long before then I realised that we were a very literate and privileged family indeed. At about ten years old, rather than being starved of literature I had read *The Forsyte Saga*, although I never had the faintest notion of what 'to let' and 'in chancery' meant.

I envied Lady Anne her governess and wondered why fate had never thought to reverse our roles. If she felt it her duty to enlighten me, I had no objections. I stopped pretending and laid my ignorance quite bare before her. She often referred to the lower classes in much the same way as Hilda referred to liberty-takers, but if she had any assumptions about colonial students, whom she probably put in a special category, she never betrayed them to me.

She expected the students to disagree with her, to heckle her and to introduce civilised controversy into confrontations with her. It saddened her that only a few of us could argue without quarrelling and she was dispirited when anyone voiced hatred of the British, in particular, and of the Empire in general.

'Admittedly, we are hypocrites,' she declared, 'but we are not intolerant. There is no intolerance about hypocrisy, only insularity.'

In her dealings with students she was sorely tried. She sometimes became so irritated by their anti-Empire aggression that she might write cryptically 'Trousered Ape' on a report, but then, undergoing a sudden change of heart, would add: 'No, not really – rather a nice young man.' I collected several crumpled and telling bits of paper of this nature. She prepared and rehearsed her speeches with considerable thoroughness, consulting reports and records in order to get the facts correct.

'It's no use doing anything, if you're not prepared to put *beef* into it!' she stated in one of her more down-to-earth moments.

In order to simulate heckling, she sometimes rattled a nut-cracker in a silver-plated dish as she practised her speeches. At other times she slapped her desk with a battered copy of *Jane Eyre*. For more realistic heckling she relied on me, and I failed abysmally. At various points in her speeches she would exhort me to 'come in with vigour and interrupt'.

'Verbally froth with anger!' she would advise, but self-consciousness made me completely inarticulate.

At the end of each day with her I realised afresh that I belonged in a cultural no-man's-land. However often I had sung 'I vow to thee my country' on Empire Day in the pouring rain, I wasn't English. Brought up as we were under a faraway flutter of the Union Jack, I believe that at that time we West Indians did think of ourselves as English. But Englishness, I now realised, contained elements of history, culture and perception to which I could lay no claim. I wasn't African either. I was of the gener-ation of West Indians who regarded 'Africanness' as something morbid – a backward step that must be avoided at all cost. Until my twentieth birthday I had never seen an African outside my school textbooks. When I dined with an African student from the Agricultural College in Trinidad I'd found myself wonder-ing if *he* really ate people as the schoolbooks said.

Lady Anne laughed when I told her this story and remarked, 'I must admit some school textbooks do irreparable harm. I always think of school for the lower classes with some degree of apprehension!'

My time with her was indeed a revelation. Her world, which I hadn't even known existed, intrigued me. I envied her the quiet, unchanging elegance in which she lived. I understood through her the psychological acceptance of roles. I suppose she was to a great extent what I would like to have been, a civilised woman, so I didn't mind serving her. If she had called me uncivilised in terms of her own life she would have been right. What would I learn from her? I wondered. A way of feeling, perhaps. She showed me that the road to knowledge wasn't necessarily encompassed by my job of teaching. Through her I realised my limitations. I even came to understand the English conception of 'the native'. From then on, English 'arrogance' of this kind, whether printed or spoken, never really offended me. I learned, instead, to laugh at bigotry whenever I encountered it.

My friends were astounded by my work as a maid.

'Man, imagine you working as somebody's maid!' exclaimed my willowy, honey-skinned Jamaican friend Charmaine. 'Imagine you cleaning up white muck!'

'It isn't like that at all,' I insisted. 'She's a real lady. She was born to it.'

'I don't care,' countered Charmaine. 'She could have been born an angel and I still wouldn't lackey for her.'

'Well, I'd sooner be her maid than yours,' I said hotly.

All the time I worked there I never clearly understood what Lady Anne expected of me. If I showed insights which she considered sophisticated for 'a native' she rhapsodised over them, commended me highly and, while still referring to me as her student-maid, narrated every detail to her friends. If, on the other hand, I seemed to be lacking in something she considered 'elementary', she was sympathetically amazed that such a serious gap had been allowed to occur in my education.

'She's a real lady'

She constantly warned me against what she considered vulgar speech. 'One posts letters. One never mails them. It is upon writing paper that you compose your letters – never upon notepaper. This is my drawing-room. It is not a lounge.'

'I am a West Indian, my lady,' I'd protest. 'We have our own way of speaking.'

I could never really grasp how sincere she was in anything she said. She was able to laugh or cry inside without moving a single muscle on her face.

Her food habits never failed to baffle me. Food was to her a simple biological necessity. She ate anything without comment or complaint provided it was straightforward and English. I tried my best to serve her starkly simple meals attractively but this pleased her only rarely. Once I served her a fruit salad in the form of a butterfly. I made the feelers, wings and body out of pineapple chunks, decorated it with contrasting pieces of fruit and overlaid it with whipped cream. Perhaps she wasn't really impressed, perhaps she thought it just another case of 'gilding the lily', but she said graciously, 'Do me a sketch of it before it passes into the realms of the forgotten. It is so beautiful – so original. I shall speak about it when I next dine at Claridge's.'

I wondered where on earth that was, but the very next morning I saw the hotel mentioned in *Tatler*, which she read with relish. I also found it a fascinating magazine and got the taste for it, so much so that long after I'd left her I used to buy it from time to time.

I well remember the look on the newsagent's face the first time I bought a copy. His jaws sagged and he squawked, 'Now what do *you* want with that?'

Lady Anne was sometimes worried because I didn't eat what she considered 'native' food. 'Let me get you what you want to eat from Fortnum's,' she suggested. 'They cater for the most exotic and even the most alarming tastes. They pride themselves upon their wide range of peculiar foods.'

'Eggs and cheese are ample for my needs, my lady,' I explained. 'I do not like the texture of meat.'

'I would have thought atavism would have helped,' she remarked casually.

'No, my lady,' I said. 'One of my ancestors choked on someone's funny bone. My dislike of meat was the consequence.' She laughed from the heart, and told that story a thousand times on the telephone.

Despite my apparent success with the butterfly dish I could not get her to accept that food should be served attractively at all times, and that if she dined alone it was even more necessary. With a quick nod and a slight flick of a jewelled finger she would wave me back into the pantry, saying, 'Do spare yourself. It is unnecessary to fuss about non-essentials. Only the *nouveaux riches* do! Think of the masses of Africans! Do you think those starving masses look for attractiveness in their mouthfuls of scrap? Do you think the Ghetto Jews did? Do spare yourself. Fussing is so unnecessary.'

I have never fussed about anything since. Lady Anne, incidentally, loved chips and often ate them with her salmon. 'Chips are my only concession to the plebeian. I adore them. So did all my family,' she explained.

She hated modern fabrics, regarding them as 'too much of a leveller'. 'Only the high-born were entitled to wear the purple,' she told me. 'Now it is of no significance. Dress does not now relate to station. In former days dress was indicative of profession, trade and station.'

Quite forgetting her professed weakness for chips, she always blamed potatoes for the Irish problem. Since I hadn't studied English history at school I knew only vaguely about Cromwell and the Irish. I told her so.

'Cromwell is not relevant,' she said bluntly. 'I am not referring to Cromwell when I speak of the Irish problem. I have in mind the sexual gusto the Irish get from the potato and its nutrients.'

I was dumbfounded.

'The other day I encountered a woman who had thirteen children,' she ran on. 'She must have been pleasured with alarming frequency!'

On days when she did not write speeches or answer letters she ritually exercised her mind. It was quite a deliberate act. First she would ask me to plump up her cushion and then she would sink slowly into a large over-upholstered chair. Next she would put on a boudoir cap to prevent chemicals in her blue rinse from harming the ancient fabric, and then I would hand her her glasses and a big black book. I cannot now remember the title, but it contained some harrowing pictures of nutritional diseases in tropical countries.

'Are you acquainted with this one?' she would ask, pointing at a man with angular stomatitis, or some embarrassing disease.

'Yes, my lady.' I shut my eyes at the sight and the memory. 'But it could be cured quite quickly with proper feeding – I've seen it happen.'

I had worked on the UNICEF supplementary food programme at home and had been delighted when our school

was chosen for an experiment. Some children were given pow-
dered milk and vitamin tablets, others were tested and treated
for hookworm and kwashiorkor. The change in some of the
children had been almost too remarkable for belief. I watched
eyes change from bleary to bright and saw attitudes alter from
lethargic to positive. I watched new work habits emerge and
new desires flourish – all through supplementary feeding –
and I became convinced that much of the backwardness in our
schools was nutritional in origin . . .

Beryl at training college in British Guiana, teaching children as
part of a UNICEF nutrition programme, 1947

I felt like enlarging on all this for the possible benefit of my
employer but I should have known better. As was usual in these
self-educational sessions she had closed the book after a few
minutes with a sudden thud and gone off to sleep.

While she slept I did the darning. I hated darning and took
ages over it. She wore very thick Lisle stockings and I endlessly
darned the old pairs. I wondered what my mother, who always

wore immaculate stockings, would think of Lady Anne's.

Or, indeed, of Lady Anne. Come to that, what would Lady Anne have thought of her? For I knew now that the Englishman's curiosity about the unfamiliar was often tinged with mockery and mistrust.

After I had left at the end of my time with her, she invited me to lunch at the British Empire Reading Rooms in the Strand. When I got there a note was waiting for me. It said, 'You must excuse me. I have been called away quite unexpectedly. Colonel Manson-Trot will take my place and I'll be back for coffee.'

The British Empire Reading Rooms were then the true haven of old colonial servants and Empire worshippers of various sorts. It was crowded, when I arrived, mainly with retired colonial servants, expatriates on holiday and coloured guests. The women wore crumpled cotton dresses they had not bothered to press, or mannish tweeds and hats, and sensible shoes. They spoke in a way peculiar to colonial servants.

'I cannot understand why so many of our overseas servants speak in that extraordinary fashion – their words are trapped between their teeth like nails in a vice,' Lady Anne had once remarked. 'I expect it is born of the fear of swallowing noxious tropical insects. It is a pity that such a manner of speaking remains with them for the rest of their lives.' I could still hear the rustle of disapproval in her voice, and I added soundness of deduction to all her other virtues.

Across the room a few coloured guests listened to their English mentors with uncommitted eyes and uncertain smiles. I read the note again. Who was Colonel Manson-Trot, anyway? How was I to know him? I decided to find a seat and wait.

Before I could make myself comfortable a voice boomed at me from an armchair almost tucked away behind heavy, faded maroon curtains.

'Lady Anne's guest, I presume,' said the voice, and almost as suddenly a man approached me with a very peculiar gait. First he took a large step with his right foot and then two quick ones with his left to bring it into line. After a minute or two it dawned upon me that he was very lame in his right leg. He could not bend it at all.

My gaze moved from his leg along his dapper body to his grey-blue eyes, and finally to his face, which had been restructured by pain and time. Nothing, I thought, except pain could have caused such ruts and wrinkles to appear.

We shook hands; all the strength which had deserted his leg seemed to rest in his hand. His grip commanded respect. There was the sagacity of a British bulldog and the relentlessness of its teeth about his handshake. He must have been a dynamic and dignified officer – but all was now dying.

'Lady Anne has been called away,' he said. 'One of her committees – couldn't be helped. You don't mind me standing in, do you?'

'No, not at all,' I replied.

'Come, sit you down. What will you have – a tropical noggin, or an English sherry – sweet, medium or dry?'

'Medium, please,' I replied. Noticing his foot sticking out in front of him like a pole, I rose, offering to get my drink.

'Nonsense,' he protested. 'There's life in the old dog yet.' He made his way to the bar and returned with the drinks, spilling a little of his beer as he handed me my sherry.

'Lady Anne calls me "timbertoes". You can see that I'm

lame, can't you?' he said, clearing the froth from his lips with his tongue.

'I hadn't noticed,' I replied. His candour embarrassed me. At home we hide our infirmities, but he was drawing my attention to his lameness. It was a fact of his life, and he was not ashamed of it. We tended to think of deformity as a punishment for sin from some vengeful God. 'I hadn't noticed,' I mumbled again.

'Then you must be less colonial than I thought. Tropical eyes age sooner than ours, they say. But since the hazards of life in the tropics are greater, I should have thought tropical eyes would be more acute.'

'I think perception is related to the level of awareness,' I said. 'It's only one of my ideas, but I think the more aware one is, the less one perceives. I didn't exactly live in the jungle. My eyes would meet your specifications if I did. Snakes weren't exactly ten a penny where I lived.'

He laughed. 'Which part of the world do you call home?'

'British Guiana,' I said.

'Hm. British Ghee-a-na,' he said. 'The French had a convict settlement near there, didn't they?'

'I think they did,' I replied.

'Have you met any French people?' he enquired, amusement in his eyes.

'I have not had the pleasure,' I replied.

'A pleasure until it happens. No guts, the French. Run like rabbits at the drop of a hat. Very odd, no stamina. Too much lavender. Cover themselves with the stuff.'

'I do believe that some Frenchmen use cologne – but lavender? This is certainly new knowledge,' I said.

'Cologne, lavender, call it what you will. They cover themselves with the stuff. I've had to stand beside them often enough – suffocating!'

I could not resist a smile. This was a new kind of dogma.

'We'd better press on. Lady Anne will join us as soon as it's possible – for coffee, perhaps.'

'What do you miss most now that you have retired?' I asked the Colonel over lunch.

'Horse-riding – I rode a lot, you know,' he began thoughtfully. 'I miss Hassan, my man – lost the knack of looking after myself. I miss the *laissez-faire*, the sense of timelessness, and of course the intrigue – glorious, that!'

It was all very much outside my experience.

'Can't get to my club often.' He was really talking to himself. 'This place is as good as any. Here we live in the past with impunity. We curse the past and yet we hanker after it.

'Are you first generation literate?' he suddenly asked. It was quite a shock – I didn't believe anyone could possibly think that of my family.

'Not really. My parents could both read. So could my grandparents.'

'Jolly good show,' he beamed. 'They had some contact with our Bible, didn't they?'

'Yes, they did.'

'Was it a translation into your language?'

'No, it was in English,' I explained. 'Our language is English – our own version of it, anyway. It differs in lots of important ways from British English.'

'That's interesting. How does it differ?' Curiosity, or concern for the mutilation of his language, brought a flush to his face.

'It differs in the sentence structure. We have retained some of the tonal implications of the African languages. We don't always use the past tense. We accent words differently. We have retained more biblical and Victorian English terms and have our own metaphors, similes and proverbs. Sometimes we broaden consonants and vowels. We also flavour our English with Spanish or French derivatives.'

'Good God!' he whispered sharply. 'Good God. There's the absurdity of the Union Jack for you. I'll fetch the coffee.' I watched him go, his mop of shaggy white hair almost standing on end.

When he returned he sat down and asked me quite calmly, 'What have you learned since you've been here?'

'I've learned a great many things,' I said. 'That newspapers can sell themselves without fear of the petty thief, that four o'clock means four o'clock, that appointments and agreements must be kept, and that milk does not have to be boiled.'

'This is extremely pleasing to me,' he said with solemnity. 'There is so much to learn in this great country of ours.'

I nodded.

Lady Anne approached our table carrying a cup of coffee. 'Apologies,' she said. 'An unexpected circumstance arose like a monster from the depths. But I'm sure Colonel Manson-Trot managed admirably.'

The Colonel shook hands with me. 'Goodbye,' he said. 'Goodbye. Count yourself lucky that your allegiance is not to the French. No stamina, the French.'

Lady Anne watched while he collected his coat and his cane. 'The dear man,' she mused. 'Priceless. A collector's piece.' She smiled at him and he bowed stiffly and shuffled away. Before I left her she said, 'They will deliver to you from Harrods a little package. Accept it as an expression of my good wishes.'

All the way home I tried to think what the package would contain. I knew whites. They presented their cast-offs with great ceremony and accepted heaps of gratitude in return. Sometimes it was something such as a Bible which in their opinion would civilise and enlighten the receiver. I'd told Lady Anne I'd never seen or owned a golliwog before coming to this country. Perhaps she'd send me one. Perhaps it would be something exotic like frogs or sugared ants.

At last the great day dawned and the package arrived. I felt quite important having something delivered to me from so grand a place. Tearing off the wrappings I dipped into the beautiful box and felt a delightful kittenish softness. Inside was a pale cream angora twin-set. I was deeply touched by the thoughtfulness that had gone into the choice of such a splendid present.

I read with sorrow of Lady Anne's death some years ago. I had learned much from her, especially an awareness of quality, both of spirit and mind. Despite all my affection and respect for her I had to admit that she had been an eccentric, but although she had great privileges, hope and charity had touched all her endeavours. Paradoxically, I learned from her not to put faith in things, or possessions, as props. In her I saw illustrated one particular truth – education could and should develop many facets of the mind, and it was quite possible to become an educated person without ever going to school. This discovery was to affect my whole attitude to the children I taught thereafter. Above all, during the months spent with her I found my own identity – learning how important to the development of my personality and my future purpose was a knowledge of the history of both family and country. I learned too the value of service and the ability to view life objectively.

5

'One black teacher'

_____

One morning the following spring, I walked down paths banked with daffodils. Beyond the North London cemetery lay a road which was to lead me to the school. My chance had come at last!

There was a kind of glory about this – my lucky day – although the grass still held beads of early rain. As if to salute my success full-bellied, fresh-scoured clouds scudded across skies of postcard blue, and pale sunshine touched the throats of blackbird and sparrow at play again after the sudden shower. The daffodils stirred as if in response to some inner harmony and my heart danced with them. Was it such a field of daffodils, so pure and so tender in their beauty, that inspired Wordsworth's immortal poem, which now had new meaning for me?

I forgot how badly the day had started. Summoned without warning to the Divisional Office from which teachers were sent out to the various schools, I arrived keyed up and anxious. My mood worsened as the morning wore on. The waiting-room was like that in a railway station but without a loo. It smelt of rain-soaked clothes and cigarette smoke. I stood in a far corner – the only black person there. Coloured teachers were a rarity. There was no one in the room that I knew. No one smiled.

'God,' I said. 'One Black Teacher. Why am I here?'

The man nearest to me thought I'd spoken to him. I said that I was just thinking aloud.

'You a teacher?' he asked in a heavily accented Australian voice.

'Trying to be,' I said. 'Been trying for months.'

'Tryin' to be too,' he said. 'Came over last week.'

Men predominated. They seemed to come mainly from the white Commonwealth. Some were openly curious about my presence and did not hide their curiosity, especially when they heard me speaking in English.

Two clerks were busy at the telephones, talking to schools about their requirements, but both men ignored me. The noise increased as the trickle of teachers arriving became a torrent. But still, despite my early appearance, I seemed to warrant no attention.

One clerk scowled at me, and then as he realised that I'd seen him scowl, his expression changed into an uneasy half-smile. The other one wagged a reproving finger at him. Was there hope with this one? I moved towards him but at once he said, 'Now let's take our time, shall we, miss, please?' in tones intended to suppress any query or complaint.

Later, as I stood tingling with irritation, I heard him wheedling on the telephone. 'Yes, this teacher here is very well qualified, most qualified. But she's coloured – I have to tell you that she's coloured.'

It was always 'but she's coloured'. And every time he notched up another failure he smiled sadly but sweetly at me.

It was more than two hours before he found me a school . . .

'Now, it's not far from here, miss. Only a sixpenny bus ride. Catch a bus going north and get off at the garage. Make your way from there. Good luck to you. You can't miss it. Really you'll have no trouble finding it . . .'

'What are you talking about?' I asked him innocently. 'Finding good luck or finding the school?'

His excessive talking revealed his urgent desire to be rid of me. I was his biggest problem by far that day. I could see it *was* a problem. He had to keep telephoning Heads who didn't really want to know about a coloured teacher. He'd found one at last who'd raised no objections but, of course, that didn't take into account her staff. All that was to come.

I forced him into the position of explaining. I wanted it clear and above-board. 'Well,' I said, 'thank you for your efforts but how about my queue position and all that? You know, one of the first here and yet last away?'

He breathed heavily, shook his head once and then began fingering the pencil behind his ear.

'Well, let's face it, miss. We wanted you to go where you'd be welcome. Teachers are like everybody else in society. They've got the same proportions of Yeses, Noes and Don't Knows when it comes to . . .' He trailed off into an uneasy silence.

'When it comes to colour,' I felt like nudging him. But what was the point? He was off now on his farewell spiel. 'Good luck to you, anyway, miss. I'm sure you're going to make a fine ambassador for your people.' I was to hear a lot of that one from then onwards. It was like carrying an unfair weight in a highly competitive steeplechase.

The weight seemed to increase when he said, 'Don't forget now, miss – you'll be the only coloured lady teacher north of the river.'

I'd got a job, I'd got a chance, and it had happened so suddenly, like the spring. After months of dreary work as a cook since leaving Lady Anne, I'd been on the point of packing a rucksack and going off potato-picking with a bunch of students. And now, just ahead of me, lay a school . . .

I stopped an old gentleman to find out exactly where it lay. He seemed very happy just to be alive, to have been preserved, for such a day.

His head was bent low and he greeted the sunshine with an odd, droning buzz of sound.

'Nice day,' I said. 'Is there a school near here?'

'Yes, very, very,' he said, and then, as if to put it beyond all question, 'very.' And immediately he was on his way again, continuing his singular song.

As it turned out, I needed no directions. I came abruptly upon the school, aged, massive and uninspiring from the outside. It was a Catholic school and I was to teach infants. That was all they had told me about it.

But when I went inside, the brightness and order, the clean colours of children's painting, the chanting of young voices, all made me feel a quickening of the heart and a renewed desire to teach.

A nun opened a door. She didn't seem in the least surprised to see me.

'I'm from Divisional Office,' I explained.

'Oh, yes,' she said. 'I'm Sister Consuelo, the Headteacher here. Welcome. Come, off with your coat and I'll take you to your class.'

She stood aside for a moment and looked me over. 'You're not coal-black,' she said, but in such a way that it carried no prejudice. She was merely stating a fact.

'I want a good teacher,' she went on, 'and I'm sure you're that. Now come along, I've got paints and paper ready for you . . .'

She had a voice as lovely as a bell. She moved, in easy strides, with conviction and vitality. Her skin was neglected but her features were strong. It was the sound of her voice, however, that attracted me then and still haunts me now.

'Here you are,' she said, suddenly stopping outside a classroom. 'These are the seven-year-olds – forty-two of them. I don't think they're *all* here today. Now, if you want anything you'll find Mrs Burleigh on your right and Mrs Rilson on your left. I must fly now. There are dozens of people waiting to see me.'

But Sister Consuelo, grossly overworked, had neglected to do one important thing. She hadn't told the class that their new teacher was black.

So when I opened the squeaking door and the class came face to face with me, there was a gasp of terror, then a sudden silence. A little girl broke it with a whimper. Some children visibly shook with fear, and, as I walked across the room, the whole lot – except for two boys – dived under the tables.

The first boy – I was soon to know him as John – perky, small for seven, and dark-haired, sat rigid on his chair, his arms tightly folded, his eyes glued to the ceiling. The other sat bolt upright.

'See,' he chirped, '*I* ain't afeared!' The freckled face, thick, tousled blonde hair and decaying teeth gave him a kind of appealing waifishness.

The others, however, all remained in hiding. Somehow, I had to lure them out.

Instinctively I walked towards the blackboard, cleaned it noisily and started to improvise, and illustrate, a story about a pond in spring.

There was a pond,
A very big pond,
That, one spring day, sighed and cried
Oh dear, oh dear, oh dear, dear, dear,
Why does nothing live in me?
No fishes, no ducks, no butterflies.

'Butterflies don't live in ponds,' someone corrected.

'Newts do,' said a voice from under a table. 'Are you the Bogeyman's lady?'

'An' tadpoles do,' came another. 'I know where there's tad-poles.'

'Come out and tell me,' I said, without turning round.

'All right, Miss.' I looked down at a little bespectacled chap.

'My name's Georgie,' he said. 'I like nature things. I find 'em up the bomb site.' He peered up at me short-sightedly. 'Miss, 'ow do you know when you 'ave to take a bath?'

'Help me to paint the pond, Georgie,' I said, 'and then we can put it up on the wall. I take a bath every day.'

'Cor – every day? I'll paint, Miss.'

'I'll help, I'll help,' came from a chorus of eager volunteers.

'Tell you what,' I suggested. 'Think of some other places where people and animals live and we'll paint those as well.'

'Well, let's do 'ouses, then,' cried a voice close beside me.

'Who are you?' I asked.

'I'm Judy Garland,' she replied gaily. Her head was smoth-ered with clips, slides and ribbons of all colours. Round her neck was a long green necklace, and a string with a key attached. Her name was indeed Judy Garland.

'You're all dressed up, aren't you?' I remarked.

'Me sister puts 'em in me 'air – she's daft, so I let 'er,' Judy said apologetically.

'Liar,' another voice countered. 'She ain't got no sister to save her soul. Truth once, truth twice, truth to last all the days of your life. You can go to Purgatory for them lies.'

At once I felt the religious influence wafting in like a whiff of incense at Easter.

'No, I won't,' Judy protested. 'I'm only playin'.'

'Do you like having all those slides and clips on your hair?' I asked.

She nodded.

'Well, that's all right with me. You'll have to wait and hear what Sister says, though.'

'Please, Miss, may I feel your hair?' she asked.

I let her.

'And me, and me,' said all those nearby.

'It's silky, ain't it? It's soft, smells lovely it does.'

'I wish I 'ad it,' they commented.

'Tell you what,' I said. 'Let's make some dolls out of rolled-up paper. Then we can give them all different kinds of hair.'

The children set to work and soon we had a very good, if crudely made, set of rolled-paper dolls, with hair of varying colours and textures.

I was soon to find that in order to prevent droves of curlered, scarfed and carpet-slippered mothers from making a daily assault upon my classroom, it was better to show myself off, like royalty, before the morning bell was rung. Then the children, their voices full of excitement, would exclaim, 'See, Mum, told you she was black!'

Sometimes they varied it to, 'Mum, Mum, choklity my teacher is, ain't she?'

'Why so much excitement on my account?' I asked Mrs Benn, the school help, who hardly ever smiled and ruled the roost whatever the time of day. Her tasks included issuing the stock, making the children drink up their milk, and mending cuts and bruises. Her spare time was spent retouching her face, which was already coated with powder, until it had the look of a mask. From time to time she would draw her lips into a more self-acceptable shape.

'To be expected,' she said. 'They'll get used to you.'

She pressed her new red lips together, distorting her mouth to add the finishing touches, and out of one corner continued, 'We only see the big black men down by the docks – never the women. The men go after our girls – the not-so-particular girls, you know. Them that would have 'em. Big and black the men are. They hypnotise the girls. Black people, real black people, mark you – not brown like you – make me scared. I touch me crucifix before I pass 'em.'

I shook my head. Did I conjure up black deeds, black ingratitude, blacklegs or black-hearted villains who ran the black market? These thoughts haunted me. How I hated that word 'black' and the emotions, concepts and associations it aroused!

Sister Consuelo, whom the children called Sister Cons for short, was a busy Headmistress, but nevertheless found time to visit the classrooms, bringing with her a genial disruptiveness. She taught music and country dancing and her swirling ebony-black habit, caught at the waist by a girdle of cord from which dangled a crucifix, rather startled me when I first encountered her dancing in the hall. She never raised her voice in anger yet one only had to threaten a visit to her office to bring about a complete transformation in even the naughtiest child. I never found out exactly how she did this. Perhaps it was because the children were so certain of her love that they always wanted to please her.

There was certainly no love in the methods of Mrs Burleigh, either in handling children or dealing with me. In me she found a ready-made enemy.

When I picture that staff-room now, through all the intervening years, it is Mrs Burleigh, staunch Catholic, who still stands out like some figure in a stern, admonitory religious painting. Mrs Rilson, small, grey and twittering, good with children but timid with adults, gives that painting some relief. And good old no-nonsense Mr James, a sort of friendly dogsbody, who had no time for either of them, remains with me as another sort of foil. He made the tea after lunch, spoke his mind on all matters and played desultory football with the boys when the mood took him. He taught the top class.

Mrs Burleigh disliked most children, cats, Jews, foreigners, and Mr James, who opposed her heavy-handed grip on her class. She railed about her pupils' evil ways incessantly. Their misdemeanours were her major topic of conversation, and no one defended their interests except Mr James.

'They are not convicts on hard labour,' he'd say. 'They didn't give you your horsy neck and dead-fish eyes. Yes, your thyroid glands are squiffy, we all know – heard it a million times – but it doesn't give you the right to be sadistic and tormenting.'

Mrs Burleigh had a special supplementary list of sins and the children listed their trespasses in one of three categories:

mortal sin, sin and 'Miss Burleigh's sin'. All teachers were called 'Miss' by the children. Mrs Burleigh's capacity for catching wrongdoers did not, however, prevent them from fighting back in their own way.

They painted her frequently and commented to each other, 'This is Miss Burleigh with a witchy face.' 'This is Miss Burleigh in Purgatory.' After we had been on a visit to the zoo, Judy giggled, 'This is midges stingin' Miss Burleigh on her bum in the penguins' pen.'

I often saw the Devil in Mrs Burleigh's face and frequently heard him in her voice. She never once treated me as a colleague or credited me with any kind of teaching know-how. This didn't worry me a bit. As far as her teaching ideas were concerned, they reminded me of a donkey-christening back home.

The poor donkey was tethered to a post by three or four feet of stout rope. Each time its name was shouted it was whacked with a stick. After a dozen or so blows, the donkey reacted to the sound, and it was assumed that it understood its name. In like manner these children were verbally tethered to their seats and punished by smacks, jibes and sneers for breaking Mrs Burleigh's rules. No parent, as far as I knew, ever protested. Like their children they accepted the punishment as an act of God. Some parents even praised her strictness but to me she was simply a bullying adult.

She was violently against research. Research, especially educational research, threatened the future of Britain, she declared. All the famous psychologists of the day were raving lunatics who practised academic cannibalism, by devouring all that was sane and good in English education.

'I'm not the slightest bit interested in reading the trash they write,' she declared. 'What has reading trash to do with teaching, anyway?'

Mrs Burleigh thought I was endangering the children's eleven-plus potential and wanted the five-year-olds streamed into good, bad and indifferent. Her mind was hermetically sealed.

I often wondered if the children were, in fact, encouraged to echo her animosity. I still remember how each time the school said prayers for pagan lands, or for the conversion of the heathen, the children would open an eye each and turn round to peer at me. I fancied, at such times, that I caught Mrs Burleigh's lips twitching in approval, her beady eyes softening a little as she crossed herself with more decorum than usual.

So much ignorance, so much prejudice, seemed to be built into the school curriculum. Once a year, without fail, the children 'saved black babies'. They paid half a crown each, chose a name for the child, and were given a photograph as a token. They showed me the photographs, exulting, 'Cor, look, Miss! I've saved a black baby.'

Or, as one seven-year-old put it to me, 'Yeh! Nah the poor little bleeder won't be a pagan no more.'

Mrs Burleigh examined me severely on questions of health and hygiene. As far as she was concerned I was a carrier of fearful tropical diseases.

'Have you been vaccinated against the smallpox', she asked me once, 'or have you had it? In your part of the world it's as common as snakes, isn't it?'

'Did you notice that speck of wet on the floor in the loo, Mrs Ril?' she would begin. 'Did you notice? Dribs and drabs all over the place!'

Poor Mrs Rilson would reply by accelerating her knitting speed.

'There never used to be specks of wet on the floor in the loo. Now we've started having specks of wetness like polka dots on a summer frock all over the place. Disgusting, I say it is. There must be gremlins with foreign habits in this school.'

'Put a sock in it. I'm sick to death of your nonsensical yapping,' Mr James would protest. 'No one here spends a penny through a garden sprinkler. The drips are out of your mouth – it's always open.'

His candour and her compulsive commentary about specks of wet amused me. Why didn't she say urine if that was what she meant? What was the purpose of the modesty?

I wasn't involved in the appearance of specks in the lavatory. I couldn't be. I walked each lunch-break to the Tube station with my penny, whatever the weather.

My visit to the Tube station lavatory was a social one; I was always greeted with a cheerful, 'Hello, love – nice and tidy for you.'

The attendant was concerned with hygiene in a positive and impersonal way. With Mrs Burleigh it was always a matter of personal accusation. For instance, there was her long vendetta about teacups.

I'd only been a few days at the school when she asked me, pointing to a cup, 'Don't you think you ought to bring your own? We haven't extras, you know.'

Rather than trouble them I bought myself a pretty cup with pink and grey flowers. Everyone else remarked upon the poshness of my cup, but Mrs Burleigh, at first sight of it, said, 'There's no need for you to show off, you know.' And when a supply teacher joined our lunch-break one day, she leaned over and warned her, 'Don't touch it! That's hers!' as if saving her in the nick of time from some poisoned chalice.

Once, when we were alone, she turned to me and said in low and serious tones, as if it were something that could no longer be left unsaid, 'You're not one of *us*, are you?'

'No,' I told her. 'I'm not English and I'm not Catholic but I'm a cracking good teacher. And that's what it's all about. Isn't it? They're short, you know – the whole world over. Ask anyone who really knows.'

I expect I aggravated her. She was middle-aged, and a bit of a fossil, and I refused to give her the satisfaction of showing any hurt or ill-feeling. I smiled at her most times. Always she looked for stereotyped 'black' reactions. Where was my Negro volatility? Where were the angry whites of my eyes? She got no answers.

She had a good friend in Mr Devillin, the 'school-keeper' – a sort of general factotum and custodian of the bits and pieces. He prowled around the school with his books, examining, querying. He had a very good opinion of himself and his work. He was devoted to his daughter Jane, who was in my class and on occasions tried me sorely.

Jane was a pale child with wispy strands of blonde hair and milk teeth decaying near the gums. She went absent at the drop of a hat but when she was in school her father visited her frequently.

'And 'oo is the guvnor then? And 'oo is the boss?' he would say.

'Yi yam, then,' she would giggle in a baby voice. She always added 'then' to everything she said, like a full stop. After kissing her noisily he would back out, smiling. He never seemed to realise that her feet were meant for walking. As soon as the play-bell went he would appear from nowhere to carry her on his shoulder wherever she wanted to go. From her perch she would look down at me and murmur, ''Ello, then.'

If for any reason at all she got into difficulties he expected me to ooze sympathy and concern. But he never hesitated to tell me, 'I'm not for 'er 'avin' a foreign teacher. I was in India, you know, during the war I was. Seen some sights, I did. None of them was teachers. Beggars, yes – loads was beggars. I seen 'em with me own eyes. Such things I seen!'

It was obvious that he thought himself belittled because his child was taught by a black teacher so I never bothered to comment, but one morning I said, 'Look, I've no time to spare. You and your daughter together are entitled to exactly one forty-second part of my available time.'

'That's not much, is it, dear?' he replied. 'My Janey 'as to 'ave more than that to pass 'er eleven-plus.'

There was one teacher who never came into the staff-room. She dwelt in a self-imposed exile that was much to the gratification of Mrs Burleigh.

Her classroom was a deep cavern under the stairs. The windows were inaccessible from the inside and impregnable from the outside. There was naturally a stuffy odour all around the room, and yet it often seemed to me that June, the teacher who taught in these nether regions, was the one relieving breath of fresh air in the musty religious atmosphere of the school.

The door of this cavern had to be kept open to provide some token ventilation and this was how I first saw her – peeking up, through the hole, as it were, full-blown and cheery.

'Come on down and in,' she said. 'I'm not the old woman who lived in a shoe. I'm the young woman who lives under the stairs.'

She was about my age, well built and forthright. Every time she laughed, which was often, rolls of flesh joined in the fun under her jumper.

'Haven't seen you in the staff-room,' I said, offering my hand.

'No, and you won't,' she said. 'Don't want a poker in my face and another up my back.'

She wriggled a finger. 'You see,' she said, 'no ring – and it shows. I'm supposed to have pinched the bloke I'm living with – and I'm not the sort to keep secrets. But what a load of rubbish! As if you can pinch men. They go where they want to.'

I found out that she was the most gifted teacher in that place. I watched her many times. She had an almost electrifying effect on a group of children, and parents held her in high regard. My class prayed regularly to Mother Mary to help them into her class rather than Mrs Burleigh's. Mrs Burleigh, for her part, always walked past June's class as if she expected a fantastic animal to rush out and grab her and, before she could protest, subject her to some unspeakable terror.

June, so sincere in whatever she did, became special to me. She was English in a very fine and particular way. Yet sometimes her words flowed too far ahead of her concern for their consequences and created difficulties for her.

One day she said to Mrs Rilson, who took her religion very seriously indeed, 'You don't believe in all that parthenogenesis cock, now – do you? Mary knew who put that bun in her oven. She was no Blessed Virgin.'

Beryl with staff and children at St Joseph in the Fields School
in Bethnal Green, London, 1954

It was as if what Mrs Rilson heard set her ears on fire.

'June,' she wailed, covering them with her hands, 'you have committed mortal sin.' And mortal sin, done or said in that school, had to be reported or confessed.

Soon enough June was asked to leave.

She was affronted. 'Who do they think they are, that bunch of Irish queers?' she said.

'You'll get another job, June,' I consoled. 'You're a good teacher.' From then on Mrs Rilson hovered round our classes – shouting at the children, correcting them, carping and nagging. In this way she purged them of our contamination.

By this time June and I had become more than colleagues. We both loved jiving and went dancing each week. June was transformed when she danced. The creativity which showed in the classroom was now restated in the artistry of her movements, and her well-proportioned body gave them an added quality. Sometimes her natural rhythm, spontaneity and bubbling good humour completely took hold of her and then it was easy to see how selfless she was – so ready to give of her time, her talent, her ideas. Indeed, of anything she had which others needed.

And so it was to her I turned eventually when I received a tug from the past. A letter arrived from Liz reminding me of her wedding.

'Come early so we can 'ave a little talk. Nothin' to tell, reelly. My fiancé never goes beyond 'is dues.'

Knowing Liz, I went early for a talk or anything else that might crop up.

When I arrived at about nine o'clock on her wedding day it didn't take me long to see that I would have to mount a rescue operation. The flat was on the second floor of a decrepit terrace in a side street. The door knocker was encrusted with rust and grime. No one had used that knocker for a very long time!

After much slurring and jangling of bolts and chains Liz opened the door. Yawning loudly, she smiled at me through very tired eyes. She held a slipper in one hand and gathered a faded housecoat around her with the other. Her hair was done to a turn. Her head, covered with curlers, looked like an army of strange, small creatures – all standing to attention. Her head seemed smaller than ever.

'Come in and sit down,' she said. 'I was just 'avin a strip-down wash. The water is pinchin' cold.'

There was no carpet on the stairs and my shoes made a noise like thunder when I walked upstairs. I looked around. It was the biggest mess I had ever seen. Empty bottles, packets of crisps, salt paper and opened-out hairpins littered the floor.

'We 'ad a beer and winkle party 'ere last night. We 'ad a good few winkles and the jellied eels was tasty.'

I examined a shell. I didn't know people ate cockles and winkles.

'I 'aven't tidied up yet. No sense doing it early. I'll do meself first.'

A lad of about thirteen peered round the door and said, 'Liz, 'oo thell is it? Gran wants to know.'

'You tell Gran it's me friend – the black teacher I was tellin' 'er of. She's 'ere early. Tell Gran not to 'ave 'er 'ouse fings on. I can't keep changing 'er. It's 'er best fings she 'as to get into.

'I washed 'er last night,' she said. 'It's not so long now till two o'clock.'

She removed her curlers erratically, although they must have taken her a long time to put in.

The chaos had overflowed into the kitchen. Sardine tins, half-empty cups, and saucers spewing cigarette ends lay in unsteady piles on the floor. I couldn't see Liz coping with so massive a mess.

'Is there anyone coming to help you, Liz?' I asked.

'Sue said she was coming over to 'elp but I ain't seen 'er yet. Me cousins 'ad their jobs to do. They went off. We didn't try an' stop 'em, it bein' Sat'day. They 'ave barrers, you see.'

'What about your in-laws?' I persisted.

'No, they won't 'elp. Me gran 'ad an argy with 'is mum, see, and anyway Gran's legs 'urt. What with the weather bein' so drizzly, I just 'aven't troubled much. I got a cake, though.' She said this as if she quite expected it to multiply like loaves and fishes and feed five thousand.

'How about money, Liz?' I asked again.

'Yeah, I'm all right for money.'

'Well, let's get out and buy some food. You can have a kind of buffet on that long table over there.'

'You do it, will you, love?' she pleaded. ''Ere, I'll let you 'ave five pounds – buy what you like. If Mum 'adn't kicked the bucket it would 'ave been so much better. But you're 'ere now. You'll 'elp, won't you, love?'

I was extremely touched by her remark. At that moment she seemed to be of concern to no one in the world. She handed me five pound notes as I wrote out the list of eatables. But I knew I couldn't cope on my own so I rang June and asked her to come and help. She came, bringing with her goodwill, good ideas and double the amount of energy required to put them into effect.

She brushed Gran's hair, imprisoned it in a coarse black hairnet and made her comfortable in her old armchair. Oddly enough, Gran took out her teeth to eat and then sat back in the chair pleased as punch and ready to sing the songs of her youth.

'Take me back to dear old Blighty,' she sang. And then: 'Just a song at twilight.' Her voice crawled over the room like a concertina that had suddenly gone out of tune. It made me sad just listening to her and I wondered why she talked of England as 'Blighty'. But I was brought back to the job in hand when I heard a soul-stirring sob from next door.

I rushed in and found Liz stuck in her dress. Every time she tried to wriggle free the material stretched and tore.

'I knew I was eatin' much more,' she wailed, 'but I didn't know I'd put on that much . . .'

'Take it easy,' said June, who had also dashed in from the kitchen. Despite all our efforts the dress split under the arms, but Liz finally wriggled into it. She was so confined, her breathing came in loud, rapid puffs. June, however, was never short of resourcefulness.

'Here, you,' she called, throwing some money to Liz's nephew. 'Buy us a razor blade. I want to open this dress. You can have a treat when you come back. Hurry!' In the end June pinned Liz's veil to hide the tear and Liz relaxed.

Sue, who was supposed to come early to help, arrived in fact very late, in the role of 'grande dame' slumming. Carrying some flowers, she climbed out of a taxi and swept into the room, elegant in an aquamarine dress with an expensive stole dangling over one arm.

She gave Liz something old, something new, something borrowed and something blue, and kissed her heartily. Then they rushed off with Ron to the church. I stayed with Gran and kept her awake to greet the pair when they came back. 'You went out a "Miss" and you come back a "Mrs". God bless you, Lizzie,' said Gran.

Sue soon cornered me. ''Ere, come and share me dark secret,' she giggled. 'I got a new bloke, Beryl. An' 'e's just like you. 'E's black. 'E come to get the laundry one day and 'e touched me 'and by accident. Six sleepless nights I 'ad. Now 'e's mine and I'm 'is. I've got to watch it though,' she said after a while. 'Wouldn't do to let the world know I've got a blackie.'

'Never mind the world,' I replied impatiently. 'Does Ron know?'

''Im? 'Is world is the dogs. 'E's only 'appy when 'e's got money on a five-to-one railer that's fast from the box.' I had to laugh. Fur stole, swanky gown and flowers – it didn't make a bit of difference. The sound was still essentially Sue.

Looking back on that day I have a special memory of June, who came at the drop of a coin in a telephone box to help Liz, whom she'd never met before.

Her friendliness got her into trouble during our evenings dancing. Everyone wanted to partner her and that was how she met Delroy, a Trinidadian boy, who passed himself off as a student. He was tall, handsome and smartly dressed and he introduced himself by complimenting June the Jiver. They spent a lot of time talking and when Delroy asked her to dance with him she did.

'I'm taking my life in my hands, dancing with you,' she said. 'Let's hope people think you're something to do with Beryl.' In those days it was not the done thing for white women to dance with black men.

Delroy chatted June up. He was studying this. He was studying that. He was doing his A levels. Actually he had a job making cardboard boxes.

June, with her big heart, was ripe for Delroy's ploys. She told me how, because of his landlady troubles, she was taking him to her charming flat, which she shared with Sam, her lover. Sam didn't object but he didn't have a chance from then on.

'I want a man with some go in him,' she confided.

'Like Delroy?' I asked.

'Maybe,' she replied, 'but I'm not sure yet.'

Those were the times when some English girls were fascinated by black newcomers. The myth was accepted as fact that a black man is by nature marvellously gifted as a lover. Many girls were keen to test this theory, providing, of course, they could keep it a secret. June was no exception and very soon she talked about getting married.

It couldn't be Sam. He had a wife who vowed never to divorce him. Inevitably, she became pregnant, and at once Delroy changed. He flaunted all his male pride in his progeny – and spoke of the baby as his seed.

'You mustn't throw it away,' he insisted. By this he meant that she mustn't have an abortion. 'A woman has babies inside her what has to come out.'

'So therefore you marry her,' I said. 'You earn enough in your job.'

But Delroy, never less endearing than at that moment, merely sniggered. 'What do you mean, marry? Why buy cow when you can get milk free? These white girls like bed. I tell you so.'

June, now deep in the sulks, began to talk of abortion. Sam was sad for her but he was scared of Delroy. 'The black bastard,' he said. 'He spoilt my life. The baby'll have kinky hair and a coal-black skin, and I can't pretend it's mine.'

June took the talk of abortion into action. 'If you want to throw away my seed,' Delroy fussed, 'come with me to see Winston and Jeannie. They has a good place.'

'I'll go there with you when I'm raving mad,' June snapped. 'But you can give me the address.' After Delroy had gone, June worried that the place might turn out to be a knocking-shop.

'I'll come with you if it's a Saturday,' I promised. 'I can't take a day off school just like that.'

So one dull Saturday morning at about ten, we met at Edgware Road station and fearfully made our way to the address Delroy had given her.

It was a squalid area and the street was full of girls plying their trade even at that hour of the day. We arrived at a low, undecorated shop with sheets of newspaper covering broken panes of glass.

Over the door it said 'Ladies' and Gentlemen's Tailors'. First we met Jeannie, a white woman, well dressed, about thirty-five. There was a wary coldness about her. Then the curtain parted and a dapper black man appeared in the doorway. He shook hands with me. He had flabby hands and had obviously never done manual work of any kind. 'I'm Winston,' he said. 'The dames call me Uncle Winst out of sheer gratitude.' He laughed. Then, touching my arm, he added, 'I wish you was the one who want the doctoring. Would do it meself 'stead of Jeannie.' He winked at me and pursed his mouth in a faraway kiss.

My resentment of him churned up inside me like bile. I looked him straight in the eye and said, 'Never is a long time, chappie. But I'd rather have twins coming out of my ears than let a scented, swell-headed louse like you lay a finger on me.'

He didn't take offence, but laughed jovially. 'Ah!' he said. 'They still come crawling on their bellies to their Uncle Winst. You call me a louse. I have money in the bank!'

I couldn't stay there another minute. I went to the Tube station to wait for June. When she finally appeared, she said, 'I haven't got twenty-five pounds. I have to produce this baby. I don't care what Sam says.'

It was a brave thing to do in those days. I took her hand and said, 'All black men aren't like Delroy and Winst. Most are ordinary dependable blokes that one can rely on till kingdom come.'

There came a day when June gave birth to a boy whom Delroy promptly named Aneurin – after Aneurin Bevan, whose rhetoric at that time cast a spell over many students from overseas. 'We callin' 'im Nye for short, man,' explained Delroy. 'He's goin' to be a great talk-man.'

But by then June had had sufficient of Delroy. When he arrived at the hospital he found that she had vanished. He was left holding the baby in more ways than one. The unfortunate little Aneurin was bundled into a taxi and placed in a home.

Much later, I was to read about the downfall of Delroy, Winst and Jeannie. They all finished up in jail. As for June, she went abroad and I never saw her again.

6

'Keep your hands off me'

My life at school was clouded by an obsessive interest in my 'blackness'. It seemed that no one could forget it, and no one really wanted *me* to forget it. I was becoming heartily sick of it. It was difficult, at times, not to become the traditional black with the traditional chip on the shoulder. It could happen in a hundred and one different ways. There was, for instance, the usually unspoken implication that there was something sinister about 'black hands'. It came out into the open during a Nature Walk.

Sister Consuelo was keen on Nature Walks. Sometimes she arbitrarily sent two teachers off on one, always stipulating the route. We either had to go to a particular bomb site or to the cemetery. Some strange and interesting plants were then springing up on bomb sites and the children liked looking at them through their magnifying glasses. But, on the whole, I preferred the cemetery. It was peaceful and expansive and, in its way, a marvellous leveller. Over it hung the comforting thought that all who went there were equal.

Sister Cons had specified 'cemetery' on this occasion, and one of the other teachers led the way, flanked by two of the sprucest children. I followed with the masses, who were eating their apples and promising 'Cross me 'eart, Miss' that they wouldn't consciously tread on earthworms. This was the best sort of truce I'd been able to effect with them in my efforts to stop their wholesale murder of living things. Snails, spiders, beetles were all killed. The list seemed endless. I'd held an earthworm in my hands and pleaded its cause. For the moment its tribe were safe. Next week – who knew?

It was a lovely day. A tramp sat on a gravestone eating half a grubby loaf and relishing it. When wasps came zooming in on us the old man was immune. Apples were the attraction. Some of the children ran ahead and caught up with the other teacher and her chosen pair. Some of the wasps went, too.

By the time I reached her, she was having trouble with a wasp that had homed in on the freckles on the back of her neck. She brushed it away and scowled, but it came back again. She swiped at it with her handkerchief but now it seemed trapped in the ruffle around her neck. This was dangerous.

'Stand still!' I said. 'Try and stand still and then it won't sting you.'

'Wasps can kill!' said one of the children, cheerfully.

'Yeh – one bited a lady, my mum said, an' now that lady's dead.'

'Hold still,' I said again, 'and I'll get it off with my handkerchief.'

She looked at me and now there was real terror in her eyes. 'Don't touch me!' she shouted. 'Don't ever touch me. Keep your hands off me!'

'Sorry,' I muttered. 'It's your neck – and it's your wasp.'

She stood there, totally ignoring the wasp, still looking absolutely petrified. The tramp we'd passed earlier now came up with us and, seemingly with her entire approval, held her still, took off his greasy cap, then whacked the wasp away. His hands were much blacker than mine.

'Keep your hands off me'

The message rang out loud and clear. Rather the tramp and his filth, rather the wasp, rather even the sting of the wasp, than the slightest touch from me.

When we got back to our classrooms I began looking at my hands, almost as if I were seeing them for the first time. That night when I went out to dinner, it was an intelligent gathering but I took this new consciousness with me. At every introduction a handshake became a challenge. I dared not dance, although I loved to dance, in case some partner by look or gesture should reject my hands.

The next day I felt the same. I was nervous about picking things up. I was especially nervous when it came to buttoning up the children's coats if their parents were about.

And then, one morning, Sister sent for me.

'Did anyone get smacked in your room yesterday?' she asked.

'Certainly not. There's no need for smacks. The kids get better and better.'

'Well, Michael's mother has said you hit him and that he went home covered in bruises. I've had a look at him. There *are* bruises, you know.'

'Well, *I* didn't put them there,' I said angrily. 'I've never bruised anyone in my life.'

I went back to the class and puzzled about it. After I'd collected the dinner money I noticed that Michael still had two shillings, which he was spinning on the table. Suddenly it all became clear. Older children who beat up smaller children often paid them afterwards to lie about it.

I remembered James who served at Mass and also served up thick ears to the smaller fry.

'Michael,' I said, 'James gave you that money, didn't he?'

'Yes, Miss,' he said, and then corrected himself. 'No, Miss. Found it.'

'No, you didn't,' I said firmly. 'James was warned not to hurt you and your sister, wasn't he?'

'Yeh, well, but you know 'im. 'E gets tempers, Miss. The Devil gets in 'im and then 'e gets at us.'

'And so he paid you to say that *I* hurt you?'

'Yes, Miss,' Michael admitted finally. ''E says black 'ands like yours leave black marks . . .'

I was staggered. Those last few words hit me worse than the damaging lie. So we were back to that again? 'Black hands' from above and now from a child. It didn't seem to me a natural remark from even a bully like James. It didn't ring true. I couldn't help wondering and grieving about the adult source whence he'd picked it up.

I suppose it was only logical in such circumstances that the children began to take more than normal interest in black people. Now when they saw a black person in the streets they would come and tell me. It was rather like trainspotting for them. But when they began referring to them as 'sunshine people' or using similar terms I was first intrigued and then concerned.

One day as we crossed the street to the church hall where the children had their dinner, I noticed a jet-black man standing at the bus stop. He wore the dress of a city gentleman or perhaps a barrister. His overcoat, bowler hat, rolled umbrella and gloves matched his skin and his eyebrows to perfection. It was the first time in my life I'd seen a man who could justly have been described as black. His black shoes glinted in the sunshine, and his teeth flashed snow-white in contrast with his face as he smiled at the line of children. He was an arresting sight.

'Look, Miss,' Olivia cried breathlessly. 'There's a coloured man, with coloured clothes on. 'Is 'at's coloured. 'Is shoes is coloured and so is 'is umbrella. Cor, Miss, 'e's ever so coloured.'

'He's a black man, dear,' I told her. 'He's nothing else.' Later I told them all, 'If black is the word you use, then I'm black and you must say it whenever you like.'

What was behind it all? I wondered. Had they been told to spare my susceptibilities? I doubted it very much, when I thought of the adult influence around them. Had I been 'touchy' at some time or other about 'blackness'? Children have the keenest nose for every nuance of hidden feeling. Or was it just a show of their own sense of what was just and kind? They certainly wanted to pour on the comfort.

'Some black fings is noice, Miss,' said Tony, one of the two bold-hearts who hadn't dived under the tables at first meeting. I'd found out by now that the 'waifishness' I'd initially seen in him was deceptive. He was a toughie.

'You're noice and you're black, ain't you?' he added. And then, warming up, he continued, 'So is Sister Cons's clothes – them's noice and black. So is me mum's new shoes and so is me p'lice car.'

'Coal is black and it keeps ya warm,' said Judy decisively. 'It makes nice pictures, too – when it's flamin'.'

In their ways, I thought, they were doing their best to adjust and it was difficult for them, for it was quite obvious that they had already been conditioned to consider anything that wasn't English as downright laughable.

I did my best to release their imaginations, to get them to see underlying causes for actions which appeared strange and ludicrous to them.

I showed them pictures of houses on stilts – the kind we have in some parts of my homeland. Although they found the pictures 'funny', they failed to discover a reason for the stilts. We therefore performed an experiment. Putting our cardboard-box house on lolly sticks in a shallow tray, I poured some water round it. At once the children understood.

'Stilts'd stop 'em from gettin' washed away,' shouted Tony.

'An' all their clothes wouldn't get soakin' wet,' observed Georgie.

'Yes,' I explained. 'It is like that in my country. Sometimes the water floods the land and the stilts help us to keep dry.'

Soon they found reasons why their 'sunshine people' wore little or no clothing, and why Eskimos wore furs; why some people ate potatoes and others rice; and why they had, themselves, fires in their homes in wintertime. It was hard work getting them to wonder why, and to question their own actions, habits and customs.

I came into my classroom one day and found Tony staring up at the electric light.

'Miss,' he said, 'early man didn't 'ave no 'lectric light. I wonder what 'e 'ad.'

'Find out,' I said. 'Why not ask your dad?'

'I asked me dad,' he reported later. ''E said cave-people rubbed stones togevver, but I'm such a bloody sod I'd rather frow 'em.'

I realised then that the 'enlisting parental help' concept wasn't necessarily what it was all cracked up to be.

Beryl with the girls of St Joseph in the Fields, 1954

Mrs Benn, the school help, lipstick already half out of hand-bag, said to me dryly, 'Parents are askin' Sister to put their kids in your class, you know. Seems they like 'em in 'ere with you.'

Ah! That was encouraging. Certainly things were going well in the class – at least as well as could be expected. I remember how at last I'd got two arch-rivals, two vitriolic little girls, to make an uneasy peace.

The normal tenor of their conversation had been:

'My mum says I ain't to sit on anywhere after you, 'cos you're dirty underneath!'

'Yeh? Well, my mum says your mum ain't been up the Baths for five weeks. She don't know 'ow your dad can stand it.'

Lately there had been a lull on this particular front.

I was half hoping that Mrs Benn would say that parents now appreciated the quality of my teaching. I should have known better.

'The mums say', she told me, 'that they reckon you must 'ave something special. Like I told 'em – you people from out of the bush can sometimes do wonders.'

She looked towards the ceiling in the most serious way. 'There are things in this earth that we 'ere 'ave never 'eard of.'

She crossed herself, snapped her handbag shut and sidled off.

'D'you mean I'm a witch or something?' I shouted after her.

Here we were, back again with another 'black' deviation – another for the list. This time it was our dear old friend 'that ole black magic'!

Another difficult child to deal with was Christopher, who Sister said was a 'little bit on the hard of hearing side'. I was later to discover that he was very deaf, with only minimal hearing in his left ear. But when she said, 'You have an enabling way with children,' I was happy to try to help Christopher.

The morning he joined my class he stood by the door and poured out his feelings in the nasal mumbling of the deaf. Nothing I did could console him. He shrank away from my hands as if they were tainted. I was at my wits' end, and in a moment of anger at my inability to cope I turned to the class and said, 'He didn't ask God to make him deaf, you know. He was born that way. You must all help me to help him.'

At once the children began to talk of deaf people they knew and we listed the qualities we needed to help the deaf.

'Patience,' said Judy. 'We mustn't mind when they make us feel mad.'

'We got to learn signs,' said Danny, 'so that we can all understand what they want and they can understand us.'

'Yes and we 'ave to be kind to 'em.' This from Tony.

'We 'ave to give them our sweets and give in to 'em,' said Prissy.

As they talked I found that I did have the extra strength of will it would take to cope with Christopher. He became a challenge to us all and it was not long before the children treated him as one of them. The difference was that 'his ears were so poorly they'd never get better'.

They accepted his temper tantrums as a way of speaking and showing his feelings, of asking for help, and wishing he could talk. They included him in their play and forgave him when he hurt them. Those who hit back were made by the others to feel ashamed of their actions, although sometimes they were hardly to be blamed.

Christopher's grandparents came to the school frequently. They never said anything to me but I felt that they appreciated what I had done for him and that he had settled down and was happy in my class.

I never really expected any token of appreciation from parents. The moment we were out of school, however daft or dirty they were, they immediately crossed the road to avoid any face-to-face contact with me.

They were, on the whole, rude to most teachers, but I fancied that a few of them picked me out for especially rough treatment. One of these was Priscilla's mother. Priscilla was a small child who gave one the feeling that all natural colour had been washed out of her, as if she'd been dipped in bleach. But one wasn't to be put off by that faded look. She was a tough, wilful and cheeky member of my class.

Her mother spent a long time hanging around, waving to her through the single clear pane of glass in the door, and often charged in to shout something to her or to me or to some other child who'd touched her the previous day. Sometimes the morning name-taking would be interrupted by her admonitions to Priscilla:

'Don't do nothink you don' wan' to, Prissy. You 'eard?'

'Yeh, Mum.'

'And tha' boy what touched you, you know where, is 'e in this class?'

'No, Mum.'

'Now, don't get yourself worked up again today. You 'eard?'

'Yes, Mum.'

'Ta-ta, then.'

She was back again at four, and she made sure I heard her questions:

'What did tha' blackie do to you today? What did she do?'

'Nothink, Mum.'

'If she done anythink to you, you come and tell your mum – your mum will 'ave 'er. Why did she 'ave to come 'ere?'

Then she would give her child an ice cream, a lollipop and a handful of chocolate biscuits all together.

One morning she looked more distrustful than usual. She walked beside me, and as I reached the classroom door, she said, 'You been givin' my Prissy nightmares. She never 'ad 'em before you come. She keeps finkin' you're a monkey and you been chasin' 'er.'

'I didn't say Miss was no monkey,' protested Prissy from the other side of me.

'You did!' shouted her mother. 'You couldn't 'elp it. You was 'avin' your nightmares.'

'I wasn't.'

'Keep your hands off me'

'Yes, you was! You 'ad your 'ands over your eyes, shoutin', "That monkey is chasin' me, Mum!"'

Prissy was by now very close to tears.

'Please will you leave,' I said. 'You shouldn't be here, really.'

'I go where I please – and I wouldn't be 'ere if my kid wasn't,' she said as she banged the door shut and walked out.

Two days later she was back. It was the same story with more venom than conviction.

'You been givin' my Prissy them nightmares again. I don't want 'er to 'ave 'em.'

'Come in,' I said.

The children were quietly writing their 'news'.

'Children,' I said, 'I'm told that little Prissy doesn't know the difference between me and a monkey. What's the difference?'

'You don' eat nuts, for a start off,' said Richard.

'Or climb trees and scratch yourself,' said the pert Olivia.

'You don' 'ave a face like one, and you learn us good 'ow to read and that,' said Maureen.

'An you smell noice – better'n my mum. She smells of Guinness and fags,' said Tony. He got on his feet, for ever the stalwart, and squared up to Priscilla's mum. 'Aw! Why don't you go 'ome?' he asked her. 'You're a daft one.'

'Yes, Mum,' pleaded little Prissy. 'Go on 'ome.'

Outgunned, Mum rushed out of the door. I slumped down in my chair, a bit bewildered by it all.

The children came crowding round me.

'Aw, poor Miss,' said Tony.

'Your mum's 'orrid,' said Olivia to Prissy. 'She goes round the 'ouses tellin' on people and 'avin' a go, my mum says.'

For weeks I saw no more of Prissy's mum.

'Prissy,' I ventured finally, 'has Mummy got a job?'

'No, Miss, she ain't,' Prissy replied. 'She goes down to Richard's place an' 'as a go at 'is mum, instead.' She sighed. 'She 'as to 'ave goes at people . . .'

And then there was Sally's mother. A really large woman she was. She was civil to everyone else, but her smiles turned into a scowl directly she saw me.

Sally sat just near the door and her mum often flung the door open to give me instructions. She never mentioned my name, never looked at me, never said 'Excuse me'. It was as if she were speaking to a ghost.

'Don't let 'er do no fizzical what's-it today. She mustn't 'ave draughts on 'er. Don't 'old with draughts, I don't. Right?'

'Don't make 'er eat when she don't want none. Them school dinners is wishy-washy. 'Er mum's lovely dinners is waitin' for 'er at 'ome. Right?'

'Don't let 'er paint this week. Not a good job for a kid – paintin' an' that. Don't do no good 'cept gettin' their clothes an' that messy and 'orrible. Right?'

Sally was intelligent and capable of deep concentration. She got so absorbed in the school activities that she often went too late to the toilet, and then, of course, all the children knew she had wet herself. I often comforted her and we got on very well. She was one of those who sometimes kissed my hands because 'they was kind'.

One day she was earlier than usual, so I said, 'Did your dad bring you today, Sally?'

'No, Miss,' she said. ''E's at work.'

'Pity he didn't,' I said, 'your sums and stories are very good. You should bring your dad to see them.'

'Keep your hands off me'

That afternoon her mother bounced in and stood, hands akimbo, before me.

'Why do you want *'im*?' she asked in a shocked voice.

'Well, you see,' I replied, 'Sally's determined and bright. All she would do if you had your way is sit around. But Sally has class. I wanted to know where she got it from.'

'Wha' do ya mean?' she almost screamed. "E's a drip, 'e's a nobody. My Sally's mine. Wha' do ya mean?'

'Yes, but why don't you give her a chance? Why do you come and fuss about her? Why do you behave as if I wasn't there?'

'I'll tell you straight,' she said, 'I wish you wasn't. I'm not for 'er 'avin' a black teacher. Wha' about later on? Wha' about if you don't know subjects proper? Them mothers keep sayin' subjects is important to kids.'

But the next day it was Sally's dad who brought her to school.

"Owdyedo,' he said. He smudged his cigarette and looked round for the dustbin.

"Ow's she doin'?' he asked.

'She's a good girl and tries hard. She should do very well later on,' I replied.

"Ope so! 'Ope so!' he said. 'I'd like 'er to earn a livin' wage. I'd like 'er to get 'er share out of life.'

I nodded.

"Er mum, she ruins 'er,' he continued. 'Gives 'er a lot of 'er own way. Blames other people for everythink. You're in good company now. If it's not me – it's you. Not to worry.'

I smiled. 'You're very fair,' I said.

'It's the only way. Fair do's is the best way.'

He shook my hand warmly and left. He was the only parent who ever shook my hand.

He seemed grateful in his way for whatever I'd done, or could do, for Sally. Looking back at that dad I can't honestly say that I met such gratitude from a mum – and, of course, I saw more of the mums. There was only one real exception and she was such a sad and sorry case.

I got to know her through her pathetic twins . . .

One playtime there was such an enormous howl in the playground that I had to investigate.

'Miss!' yelled Tony. 'Look! It's the twins – it's Alfie and Bertie – they got to school at last. They been skiving at 'ome, that's what they been doin'. I ain't seen 'em since we went down the 'op fields. They was there with their mum.'

At once the children were around them in a cruel ring, poking them with one hand and holding their noses with the other. 'Cor, Miss, don't they pong! Just like they always done.'

The twins hung unkempt heads, covered their dirty faces with dirty hands and screamed.

'Stop it!' I ordered, breaking up the ring. I tried to comfort the tots but could do nothing with them. I fetched Sister Consuelo, who took them in her arms and hugged them, dirt, tears, runny noses and all.

They calmed down as she led the way indoors. 'They're yours,' she said to me eventually, 'I'm afraid they're yours.' She sighed, as much as to say that she knew she was loading me with quite a problem.

'We must remember, from time to time, in this school,' she said, staring upwards, rather like Mrs Benn acknowledging my black-magical virtues, 'that Christ washed the feet of the beggar.'

Her words were utterly out of keeping with her very real

compassion but they touched me. Then, as if she'd dutifully made a compulsory statement, she fished tissues out of her pocket and wiped their noses.

'Oh, you poor lambs,' she said, 'I wonder if you've had anything to eat at all this morning?'

Absolutely nothing, it seemed, for when she brought them large cheese sandwiches they grabbed them and ate ravenously. But when I offered them milk, after she'd left, they knocked my hands away.

Each day the twins were late at school. Their thin, tall, careworn mother brought them and left them without a word. She never came in. She just hung her head and walked away.

The twins hung their heads too. Always they'd find their own corner and cling to each other like two tiny statues. If anyone poked or teased them they'd let out a piercing shriek. If one screamed the other screamed.

Then, one day, a stray cat stole into the classroom. For the first time I saw them looking up. I watched their tear-stained eyes timidly following it around the room. It gave me an idea. Two days later I arrived in class, to a rapturous reception, with a hamster in a cage.

I walked over to the twins. 'Alfie and Bertie,' I said, 'it's *your* hamster. You must look after it – no one else.'

The next morning I felt someone furtively poking at my leg. It was Alfie. He didn't speak. He just handed me a packet of food for the hamster. I held it up high and the whole class cheered. The twins looked up. I could see the faintest glimmer of a smile on their faces.

'You done awright, kids!' patronised Tony, implying that they'd 'nicked it', as, no doubt, he would have done himself.

But when he went near the hamster they started their screaming duet again.

'Now, come on, Alfie!' I said. 'It's your hamster. Now you hold it very carefully and then show it to the others.'

Alfie took it gingerly out of its cage. Somehow the very touch of it eased him. He began stroking it and then, at last, he handed it over to Tony. I was watching Alfie. He seemed to be working up to something. Suddenly he spoke. 'Look, Tone,' he said, ''e's got a pocket in 'is face.'

The class laughed. I laughed, too. Then Alfie and Bertie laughed. They laughed until their tears came – for a brand-new reason.

'Tomorrow,' I said, 'you must give it a name. Now think about it seriously. By tomorrow I expect you to come up with one.'

Tomorrow came and it was Bertie who said, 'I got one, Miss – it's Billy.'

Those boys came to life – miraculously, I thought – through Billy. They brought him the strangest presents – cigarette cards, gobstoppers, pieces of tripe. And, in a way, they became people of substance, worthy of respect. After all, they owned Billy, whom the class doted on, and made this plain. They clung less and less. They began to go their separate ways – as much as twins ever can.

By this time I had given up taking my dinner-time break in the staff-room. My being there was a source of discomfiture. So, as June had done before me, I went into exile. I ate, splendidly isolated, in the classroom.

One day I was tidying up after my meal when I felt a strange, sad presence in the room. I turned round to see the tall, wan woman, with strangely unwashed hair, who hung her head when she collected the twins.

'Please can I talk to you,' she said. Tiredness drained her voice. Overwork showed in every pore.

'Just want to thank you', she said, 'for looking after 'em – I mean the twins. You've made such a difference to 'em. But was you told about 'em? Was you?'

I shook my head.

She sighed. 'Well, it's better you know this way – better to be told by meself. They're my sin, you see, and I'm sufferin' because of it. You see, me dad brought me up after Mum went and things 'appened that shouldn't 'ave between 'im and me. So there it is – God don't 'elp me no more. Couldn't really ask 'im, could I?

'So there's no 'ope for my boys, now – God 'elp 'em. But, as I say, I ain't got the right to ask 'im. Them boys never chose life, though – we gave it to 'em, me and my dad!'

What could I say? Nothing at all, really. It was all so wretched and absolute. But I had to say something on behalf of the twins. I had a stake in the twins.

'Of course there's hope for them,' I said. 'Someone's got to keep fighting for them until they start fighting for themselves. You know what they say – while there's life, there's hope.'

Hope? It seemed a brave word in her context – frankly, I didn't see much hope for this worn-out mother.

'Won't you see Sister Consuelo?' I suggested. 'I'm sure she'll help.'

'I can't,' she sobbed, 'I never talk to no one. But you're different. I've 'eard say that black people don't 'arp too much on the rights and wrongs of things.'

'We don't set out to judge,' I admitted. 'At least that's true of some of us.'

She had come to me, of course, for an additional reason. I was to have this happen to me over and over again. There comes a time when the terribly handicapped or grievously hurt person, with nowhere else to go, seeks the final resort of black consolation. Deep down what they're saying is, 'Now I'm on your level. When it comes to suffering and humiliation, you've been there before me. Help me, please, fellow traveller.'

7

'But love 'im I do'

The twins' mum was a rare intruder. Usually I had all the time in the world to think during those lonely dinner-breaks; to think especially about teaching. Life as a teacher in another country was difficult enough without the added complication of animosity.

Teaching at home had been simpler by far. There it had all been laid down like regimental standing orders – timetables, syllabuses, bells, work records. And as far as the teacher was concerned, it was – to borrow another image – more a matter of clocking in and clocking out like a factory worker.

There the emphasis had been on routine and the child learned by doing, which meant doing exactly as the teacher said. The teacher was expected to be as punitive as the 'good parent'. Symbols of power such as straps and canes were perfectly acceptable to the West Indian parent. The traditional pattern of child-rearing that had been handed down was 'Love the child when you can, look after him when he is ill and beat him when he is bad'.

The pattern was logically followed by the West Indian teacher and so there was the routine chanting of the alphabet, and multiplication tables, and the litany-like regurgitating of facts on strict request.

'Play' never came into it. 'Play', as part of the preparation for life, never figured in that scale of values. 'Playing' was just not accepted as a child's all-through-childhood right. Behind it all was a concept of worth through work – something that had its roots in the rigours of a slave society, and the greed and callousness of the slave-owner. A slave was beaten for 'playing'. In other words, 'playing' was akin to shirking.

I had been released from this primitive approach. Indeed, I had sought release, had applauded the new concepts of gaining the willing co-operation of children, and of trying to bring out the best in each and every child. But it was harder by far – much more demanding. I don't think that many parents realise this.

But there were always the consolations that close contact gives. The rendering up by the child of some vision, some odd angle on life, just some odd happening, that can enrich one's day. Things that can cause a teacher to reconsider adult assumptions.

Not all of them are necessarily pleasant and reassuring, as, for instance, the time when I saw the strangest side of Tony. He'd come into the class with a bunched-up look about his face. He looked quite a little gargoyle.

'Whatever's the matter, Tony?'

He spewed something out of his mouth with such force that it clattered as it rolled over the desk. I looked closer. It was an ancient pair of dentures.

'Wherever did you get them?' I asked.

'What, the ol' choppers? Found 'em, I did, Miss.'

'Yeah, he found 'em yesterday,' the girls cried in chorus. 'In Judy's garden, 'e did. Cor! They was dirty, Miss. But 'e washed 'em.'

'Yeh, I washed 'em,' Tony said virtuously. 'An' I ain't been selfish wiv 'em. I been thinkin' of others. I been sharin' 'em an' that.'

'What!' I exclaimed. 'Have you all been putting those awful things into your mouths? You don't know who they belonged to. The person might have died of a terrible disease!'

'But we washed 'em,' they all protested again.

'An' it's not rubbish,' Richard pointed out. 'Carol's mum paid two quid for 'er choppers, didn't she, Carol?'

'Please give them to me at once, Tony!'

'Oh, no, Miss, that ain't fair,' said Richard. "E found 'em and 'e wants to keep 'em.'

I thought hard. 'Fairness' was now involved. 'Fairness' was something that was frequently in their minds and talk.

'Will you all promise me that you won't put them in your mouths?'

They readily promised.

'Well, then we'll all look at them – seriously.'

"Oo ain't serious about them, then?' Tony asked diffidently. Everyone crowded around.

'They ain't 'arf different to my Fifi's teeth!' said Prissy. She nudged me. 'Fifi's my cat, you know.'

'Well, then, Prissy,' I suggested, 'you draw Fifi's teeth and Tony will draw these. Then you can compare them.'

They set to work with a will. A few days later they had made a very informative 'book', and Tony had written, 'Brush your teef every day or I will have to give you these choppers. Miss says they come from a lidi what died of diziz.'

The strangeness of small boys never ceased to baffle me. The only really hostile little boy I ever met in my long teaching career was in my class at that school. He was the same John who at my very first entrance had sat up as boldly as Tony. John had scorned to 'take a dive' with the rest of the children. But in his case it seemed to be a matter of instant hostility which became worse as time went on.

Without rhyme or reason, he used to steal up and kick me on the shin. Hurting me gave him a great deal of pleasure. We talked about fair play and hurting others and everyone responded except John. He still crept up and kicked me at every opportunity. I was at my wits' end. Finally I arranged with Mrs Rilson that she should have John for an hour. When he was out of the room I appealed to the children for their advice.

'What do you think I ought to do? John often hurts me. I don't think it's fair, do you? What would you do if you were a grown-up?'

'Clout him,' remarked Judy.

'Yeh, dot 'im one, Miss,' advised Tony.

'Kick 'im back, that's fair, ain't it?' said Olivia. 'Then send 'im to Purgatory and flamin' 'ell.' All their thoughts led towards violence.

'No,' I said, after a while, 'I've got an idea. I think I'll get a football. But don't tell John. If he kicks me again we won't let him play, will we?'

The very next day I bought a football and the ever-willing and able Mr James pumped it up for us. It was our special secret. There was an air of expectancy in the class when John came in. Everybody wanted to see what he would do. I looked away for a moment and immediately John leapt from his seat to fetch me a hearty kick.

But before it landed I caught his foot and removed one heavy shoe.

'Give me the other one, please,' I said, 'or I'll take it.

'See this,' I went on, pointing to my black, waspy belt. 'That's for judo.'

They were all most impressed. They knew all about judo. They'd heard or knew about most techniques of violence. So John obeyed and walked about shoeless for the rest of the morning. At the break I said, 'I'm now going to take the boys out to play football. But you won't play, John, unless you promise never to be spiteful again. Here are your shoes.'

He snatched them from me and hurled them on the floor.

'I won't promise you,' he said. 'Sucks to you.'

'You can tell your mummy', I said, 'that you kicked me and so I took your shoes away.'

He made the time-honoured gesture of contempt with two busy fingers and, indeed, was still working away with them when I went out of the door.

Next morning I saw a very large, very blonde and daunting woman waiting outside my classroom. With some trepidation I asked her inside.

'John told me what 'appened,' she said, 'so I brought you these. 'E said there's a six-inch 'ole in your stocking where 'e kicked you. 'Ere you are.'

She offered me some new stockings. 'Nylons are pricy,' she said. ''Ave 'em – I'll feel much better if you do. Oh, 'e's a case, 'e is.' She sadly shook her head. ''E's bad and lost.'

I really couldn't think what to say to John's mum. 'Let John bring them at the end of term,' I suggested finally. 'Yes, he did ladder my stockings. But he's all right, really. I'm sure he is.'

She looked at me, totally unconvinced, but then said the most surprising thing, 'Thank you, teacher. John thinks the world of you, you know.'

He does, does he? I thought, as I watched her broad, blonde bulk swing down the corridor. Whatever went on in the minds of little boys? If this was affection, God help me if it ever turned to hate.

The footballing went on and before each game Tony would take John aside and ask him seriously, ''Ow abaht it, then. You promise not to 'urt Miss?' And each time John defiantly shook his head, Tony would tell him, 'Awright, then, mate, you don't play.'

This continued for a full week. Then one break-time John got up suddenly and said, 'Write your name on the board, Miss. Go on. Bet you can't.'

Puzzled, I complied. Directly I'd put down the chalk John stuck out his chest, walked bravely to the blackboard and gave my name a most resounding kiss.

'I promise never to hurt Miss,' he said solemnly.

'Don't you think we ought to give John a clap for being a jolly good loser?' I asked the class.

'Yeh!' said Tony, raising one arm. 'Free cheers for a bloody good loser!' There was a faint patter of applause.

'Tell you what, though, Miss,' he said, as we went out to the playground complete with football, John and all, 'that wouldn't do for me. I'd want free cheers for a bloody good winner.'

I could see that. Tony was a natural-born winner. I've often wondered since what became of him – success of some sort, I'm sure. Exactly what sort is another matter. He was loyal, brave, perky but also extraordinarily knowing about the seamier side of adult life. He talked with surprising authority about wheeling and dealing on the black market. He talked also about 'me tater' – a weapon which, for some reason or other, he considered essential, either for security, or status, or both. I was horrified when I learned this was a potato in which a razor blade had been part embedded.

In many ways I was the innocent among those infants . . .

Beryl with the boys of St Joseph in the Fields, 1954

Spring came early. We went on an outing to Chessington Zoo. For many of the children this traditional outing was a big event. Those boys who had been wearing the same clothes all winter long knew that by outing day their mums would give them 'new' second-hand clothes from the stalls in the market. A few wore clothes of older brothers. They were quite unselfconscious and, pretending that the too-long sleeves were elephant trunks, played zoo games on the grass. Some of the children had enough paste sandwiches and currant buns to last them for a week and ate all the while they played.

It was at such times one saw the loyalty the children had to each other, the strength of their feeling for other children living in the same street and the bond of church and family. Before we climbed into the coach Tony crossed himself, closed his eyes and muttered a prayer to St Christopher, the travellers' saint, then he made the others comfortable before he sat down. After that he turned his attention to Prissy's hair, which had been home-permed by her mother. 'I don't like your 'air, looks like straw to me – crinkly straw,' he said.

'Carrots or coals, 'air is 'air,' said Danny, who had carrot-coloured curls.

'It's me perm,' said Prissy. 'Me mum done it.'

They glanced at me. It was my turn now. 'Did God fry your 'air, Miss?' asked John. 'Bubble and squeak goes like your 'air when me mum fries it up.'

I explained yet again that my hair grew the way it looked.

At the zoo they talked about the animals in the same way that they talked about themselves, using familiar language, familiar sentiments and the concepts they understood.

'Look at that ronocerous,' said Judy. 'I'm glad I'm not 'is bum!'

'Look at the giraffe,' said Tony. 'I'd like to ride 'im in the races – up the Derby.'

They were a happy group of laughing children and on the way back we stopped in some woods. They ran around stroking tree trunks, running, climbing, shouting – experiencing space and size – finding new textures, and consciously listening to the sounds of nature for the first time.

'Sparrers ain't birds,' said Prissy, 'they're Londoners.' She spoke as if she was absolutely certain of the origins of sparrows.

'But love 'im I do'

The children sat playing on the grass and I read a small book, *Experience in Education*, which I'd brought along with me. A man approached me – a flicker of friendliness on his face – his cloth cap at an angle.

'At home in these surroundings, I daresay,' he said, glancing at the trees and stressing each syllable in the way the British do when they are determined that foreigners shall understand English. I nodded vigorously for a minute or so. He reached over, took the book in one hand, ran the other over the page as if searching for a particular thing and, after turning the book upside down, he returned it to me.

Not to be outdone, I took it, sniffed it, stroked it, kissed it noisily and gave it back to him.

For a moment he didn't know what to make of me and then I said in the best Cockney I could muster, 'Over 'ere, you lot, 'ere's a nutter wot can read upside-down writing.' The man was speechless. He turned and ran off, dropping the book and stubbing his toe on a bit of wood.

'Get 'im back, Miss,' said Danny. 'I want to do 'im.'

'Yeah, get 'im back,' Judy chimed in.

'No I can't,' I replied. 'We're going back now.' They fell about laughing as Judy demonstrated how the man ran off.

On the way back I played my harmonica and the children sang simple tunes. They liked me to play even if my playing was rudimentary, to say the least. Only Tony covered his 'lugs', as he called his ears. After a little while, they got tired of singing and talked.

'Me Auntie Julie sings and plays 'er screamy violin,' said Sally. 'Me dad can do bettah with 'is bum and two spoons.'

'Me dad plays the piano,' said Seamus. ''E comes 'ome

swearing drunk and 'is money rolls round everywhere. Me dad lets us keep it. Finders keepers, he says. I love me dad. 'E done us proud.'

They told me other stories too. 'We got 'undreds of pennies up the telephones,' said Bertie and Alfie. 'We was standin' near 'em and they just come pourin' down. I 'ad to get me grandad and 'is mate.'

'It's stealing!' I said.

'No, it ain't,' they shouted. 'It was toffs' money. That's why we 'ad it.'

Everyone agreed that Bertie and Alfie had done right to do the telephones. I couldn't find out who or what they thought the toffs were – some vague entity that they must resent at all costs. They hardly showed hate, jealousy, greed or envy when they dealt with each other but they showed these traits quite readily when dealing with a specific group of people. It was perfectly all right to be nasty to Jews, Protestants and blackie sailors down by the docks.

'Miss,' said Judy, bringing me back to earth, 'I went up the black market but I didn't see no blackies there.'

'Is that where you got your coat?' I said.

'No, it come off the back of a lorry,' she said. 'Me mum can get you one, she walks be'ind the lorry and picks 'em up.'

There came the time when I felt I just had to move on, to try something else, to see if I could fit in better in some other place. There were several reasons for this restlessness.

Without June I had no friendly contacts. There was also the longing for the certainty of a peaceful day – peaceful in the sense that there would be nothing that would shake me to the core.

Shocks still came from all quarters. Some were entirely unconscious but they were just as hurtful. One of these came from Sister Consuelo, of all people . . .

I had been ill for a week and when I returned I found the whole school in the throes of preparation for Open Day. Sister had selected a poem for my class and had taught them the first three verses, complete with all the actions.

'They love it!' she assured me. 'Here it is. Of course we'll have to dress them for the part.'

She handed me a book of nursery rhymes, open at the selected poem. My heart sank. It was 'The Ten Little Nigger Boys'.

'Tell me, Sister,' I said, after I had gained control of myself and trying now to hide a smile, 'what do I do to make them look the part – paint them with boot polish to look like me?'

She put her hand to her mouth. It was her turn for shock. 'Oh, my dear, my dear,' she murmured, 'you know I just hadn't thought of you in that way at all.'

'Well, I don't think of myself in this particular way' – I pointed to the lurid illustrations – 'but who knows what the children will think of me after acting all this out?'

'You're right,' she said, 'you're absolutely right,' and she began looking around, as she usually did, for a way of turning conviction into immediate action.

'We've got to watch this – we must watch it!' she told me. 'I'm going into the library right away. There's that *Story of Little Black Sambo* and I'm not too sure about *Doctor Dolittle*.' In her mind's eye she was already ferreting out offending titles from the shelves.

'Oh, there's no need for that, Sister,' I assured her. 'That doesn't worry me. What's more important is Open Day – what are we going to do, now?'

She thought for a moment and then exclaimed, as if struck by rare and precious inspiration, 'I've got it – why don't we do a sea shanty?'

Why not? Anything was better than 'Ten Little Nigger Boys'. So we did a sea shanty, all hale and hearty, salt-sprayed and Anglo-Saxon, and there was no need for boot polish after all.

I think that during the long months I was at that school it was the religious life that finally got me down. It reminded me of rain. We were never free of it. Drizzle, shower or downpour, it always came. It was like a climate without a single sunny day. I wasn't allowed to take Religious Instruction but I had to accompany my class to church several times a week. Most of my class had a very well-developed sense of sin which delighted the priest but quite bewildered me. They were somewhat confused over God and Jesus and at times interchanged their roles. Sometimes God even swapped roles with Satan.

Some of the more nervous children were terrified by the notion of hell-fire. One seven-year-old was so frightened of meeting the Devil that I had to take her to the lavatory. ''E's red, Miss, with black spots,' she said as she lowered her knickers.

Anti-Semitism stalked abroad at Easter. I just couldn't understand this when I thought of the warm and generous Jewish family with whom I lived. They were a hard-working family, determined to succeed. My landlady was a German refugee and so she understood the nature of persecution and the disorientation that feeling an outsider could cause. She was deeply involved in the lives of students from the colonies, helping out financially when allowances were overdue, cheering the homesick, the anxious and the frustrated, and creating a strong sense of family in her home. She saw us neither as natives nor as curiosities but as people who, in order to survive as individuals in a strange land, were compelled to use their own ethnic tools, perceptions and insights.

Tony hated the word 'Jews', although I'm sure he didn't relate it to real people. At Easter he told me, 'Look at God, Miss – all bleedin'. It's because of the Jews.' At these times when I talked with the children I despaired for the brotherhood of man. The older children would 'save' African babies at half-a-crown a go and yet fervently hated all Protestants.

But they gave me a let-out. 'You ain't a Protestant, Miss – you're coloured. You'll be awright.'

Tony, in his more realistic moments, would point to a statue of Jesus in Mary's arms and comment, 'Ain't that God a soppy baby,' but the next minute, conscious of committing mortal sin and fearful of heavenly come-uppance, he would cross himself and launch into obsequious rapture, 'Ooh, but love 'im I do – love 'im I do.'

The God these children talked about seemed to me to be a selfish, pernickety, grasping old man who reacted violently when people didn't do as he wanted. But here, as well, there was confusion. The children often struck me as being quite undecided about whether to choose heaven or hell. Hell, to them, was where the action was. 'It's nice and 'ot, like where you come from, Miss,' a child once told me. In Heaven, on the other hand, there was peace and quiet – much too much of it. Few of them really wanted to go to Heaven.

Sister was loud in her praise of the way I'd coped with Christopher and a few weeks later brought me Shane, of whom she said very little. We were preparing for Mothering Sunday and I stopped and introduced him to the class, who were all making paper flowers. He joined in after snatching some white crepe paper for his own flowers. All the class had mothers at home and were making yellow flowers to take to them and he won instant sympathy with his choice of paper. We guessed that his mother was dead. It turned out that we were right and that he lived in a block of flats with his dad.

As time went on, even through his wilfulness, I found he had a quick intelligence and a sensitivity to words and poetry which belied his age, but if I showed too much interest in his writing he tore it up. He was a born hustler – with searching, keen, observing eyes. He could name every shop in the High Street and every station on the Northern Line. He never stayed to school dinner but went off each day to meet his dad outside the chip shop in the market and returned to school laden with goodies.

When I asked him where he had got them he shrugged and said, 'Up the offices,' or, 'From me Auntie Nelly.' One day a policeman came into the school to see Sister. His mother was the school cook and he had been at the school before the war. But at the sight of the law Shane was like a cat on hot bricks and eventually hid in the toilet. I knew then that he stole things from the market and I encouraged him to come into the classroom on the days when he returned early from his wandering lunch. After a time he talked freely about his mother and of his life without her.

'My dad had to keep feeding her medicines then one day she died. She went to the hospital and she never came back. I never saw her. She just died. I don't know where she is now. I don't know what they done with her.'

'Did you ask your dad?' I said. 'It's a pity you didn't go to her funeral.'

'I ask my dad if she had one of them but he never tells. He cries over her sometimes.'

One day he asked me home to tea. I was delighted and he waited for me. It was autumn and the evenings were drawing in, but Shane waited long after the others had gone to take me for that cup of tea.

'It will be a nice cup,' he promised.

We walked hand in hand towards his flat and he talked of his dad who, he said, took him everywhere. He said that his dad left him outside the pub after giving him two bob. 'Sometimes when I'm cold I put me face round the door and shout, "Dad, I'm cold." Then he comes out and gives me a lemonade shandy.'

We approached the flats, the light from the scores of windows giving them the appearance of an animal with a thousand eyes.

'Not far now,' said Shane and turned down a long concrete walk. We walked past an old bath full of coal and then up some stairs. Up, up, up we went. Five floors up. 'Not far now,' he said again. A cat ran out of the darkness and rubbed against him. His hands softened as he stroked it.

We walked past a clutter of milk bottles and piles of heaped-up rubbish and then Shane put his face to a letter-box and called softly at first, 'Dad, open the door, me teacher's come.'

Silence. Shane looked at me as if he couldn't understand what had happened.

'Dad,' he called again with mounting intensity. 'Put on the light.'

He knew his dad was out but something kept nudging him on.

'Dad! Dad!' he called again. A look of despair the like of which I'd never seen before came into his eyes. 'Me dad's out,' he said flatly. 'He said he'd be 'ere. Guess you can't 'ave the tea.'

I hugged him and he stiffened. 'Never mind,' I said, taking his hand. 'I came all the way home with you.' His hand was clammy with shame. All the panache had gone. 'What will you do now?'

'Go to Auntie May till Dad comes in,' he said with mock cheerfulness. 'Then I'll get some chips. I got two bob.' He always had two bob, it seemed.

He accompanied me to the bus stop and although his talk was as grown-up as ever I could see that there were tears in his eyes. As I went off I saw him standing there – a little figure in the darkness.

At school the next day he was extremely naughty and as he had committed one of Mrs Burleigh's sins he had to face her kind of music. He stood with his face to the wall, his fingers in his ears. As I passed him he winked at me.

I could hear the school at hymn practice again.

> Sweet Heart of Jesus, fount of love and glory,
> Today we come, Thy blessings to implore.
> Oh touch our hearts, so cold and so ungrateful,
> And make them, Lord, Thine own for evermore.

The sentimental words rang falsely in my ears. Suddenly I made up my mind to leave the school. I wanted wider experience and I would go as soon as I could.

The children seemed sorry when the time came. They brought little gifts – chocolates and cakes of toilet soap. I was going to miss them, since I always missed the children when I left a school. 'Tony won't be there to bless me when I sneeze,' I said, 'and how about you, John? Shan't be seeing you any more.'

'Aw, knickers and sucks,' he giggled, and charged from the room.

Judy, bless her, even tried to engineer a happy ending for me as far as the parents were concerned. On my last day she literally dragged her mother into the room.

'Kiss 'er, Mum,' she ordered. 'Kiss my teacher. Go on. You'll see she don't niff something 'orrible. Go on – "hug and kiss your partner".' This was a line from a West Indian sing-song I'd taught them. She pushed the bewildered woman towards me. 'Me teacher don't niff, do she?' Judy persisted.

'We was only talkin',' whimpered the embarrassed mum, her face as pale as paper. I wondered how many 'we' were, and when, and where, and how many times I'd perfumed their conversation.

'Oh, don't worry, Mrs Garland,' I consoled her. 'People can say anything they like about me. D'you know what we say at home – "A man is a labouring man when he can smell his own sweat . . ."'

I suppose I could have added, 'And God knows that I've worked like a black here!'

8

'I 'ate school'

The first moments at my new school weren't exactly what I had hoped they'd be. I arrived there on a drab day that matched the school itself, an old Victorian building set well back from the street in a mud-coloured playground. I walked up and down the street trying to find my way in, and at last saw a gate over which the letters E—R—NCE were dangling. ENTRANCE perhaps, but not WELCOME.

In the hallway a voice boomed reprimands at children, but apart from the booming voice the school was quiet. At the end of the voice I saw a middle-aged woman wearing a large, tent-like smock with a thin band around the waist. Each end of the band was tied to the wrist of a small boy. One of the boys chewed greedily at his sleeve.

'Excuse me,' I said, 'can you say where I can find the Head-mistress, please?'

'Here, just here,' she replied as if I was hard of hearing. She spoke with lapses of a second or so between the words and eyed me warily. She was a strange woman who seemed to be made up of large and small pieces and on top of the largest piece was a strong, fighting face.

'I've come from the Divisional Office,' I said. 'They told me to come here.'

Her eyes roamed over me. It was as if she was making sure that all the parts fitted exactly as she would have liked them.

'You're from Africa,' she said. 'How much English do you know?' Before I could reply she said sharply, 'Follow me.' And she took me on the most erratic tour round the classrooms, with the two tethered boys weaving in and out of the furniture. She stopped at a door, jerking the boys to a standstill. 'Here is the class you're going to take,' she said, eyeing me with palpable distaste. She watched my movements inch by inch but her doubts still lingered. In a last effort to come to terms with them, she said, 'I wish I knew about your English. I wish I could be sure.'

'The Ministry of Education was,' I said, remembering those three hatted ladies who had probed their way through the interview with me.

At this point she freed the two boys who, sighing with relief, ran clattering down the stairs. As we entered the classroom, the children made some sniggery noises, which died down when the Headmistress stood rigidly to attention in front of them. I waited for her to burst into the National Anthem but she whispered, 'I have to stare the nonsense out of these children.' Then without another word she marched out, leaving me with a huddle of whiny, chewing seven-year-olds who pinched and plagued each other the moment they felt no one was lording it over them. Suddenly one of them discovered the difference and said, 'Your face is black.' I nodded, but obviously he wanted me to do more and in a giggly sing-song he started singing, 'Fee-fi-fo-fum, Blackie bum bum bum.' The others joined in and they broke into hysterical laughter which grew from a trickle to a deluge and subsequently got quite out of hand.

'Look here,' I said. 'If you want to sing bathroom songs, sing some really good ones. Make my ears burn. I know better rude songs than that.'

'We're being naughty,' came the cheerful reply. 'You can't stop us.'

'I don't want to. Be as naughty as you like.' One cocky little boy spat in my direction, causing me to discover that he was drinking his milk out of time.

'I don't like milk,' I said. 'And do you have it before the others?' He spat some more and made a gurgling noise in the bottle before I handed him the duster. 'Go on. Wipe it up.'

'I can't,' he said, 'and I'm not going to.' I could see quite clearly that they were used to 'NO', 'DON'T', 'CAN'T', 'WON'T'.

'Babies can't,' I answered. 'Babies only make messes. Who'd like to help a messy baby?' Several hands went up, but before long I saw the offender slyly jostling the others to wipe up his own mess. The children laughed foolishly, argued about the amount of froth in their spittle, thumbed their noses at me and dared me in every possible way. They were naughty in a fascinating and creative way and once won over would make an interesting class, but the staff didn't help. When I met them, all, without exception, complained about the Head, described her as the Founder of the Bitches' Association, and accused her of having favourites among parents and children, whom they were expected to treat as if they were pieces of Dresden china. There was a feud going on between the Head and all the staff. For me, a black foreigner, this was no place to be. I made up my mind that one day in that place was enough. Just then the Head erupted into the staff-room, ignoring the dirty looks that were directed at her.

'Ah, you've met everybody, I see,' she said. Then, turning to the staff, she added, 'She's come on recommendation, the same as the other one did, but I'm taking no chances.' To me she said, 'You can have degrees pouring off you but as far as I'm concerned you're African.'

'I'm a qualified and capable teacher,' I said hotly.

She shrugged her mannish shoulders and replied, 'The proof of the pudding is in the eating.' Then she announced in a most muscular manner, 'I'm going to take a lesson in that class on the threeness of three and when I'm done with them those children will be fit for the eleven-plus.' The staff seemed to be enjoying a joke to which I was not a party and cocked snooks at her backside when she flounced out of the room on her stated mission.

At lunchtime I went back to the Divisional Office and asked for a transfer. I had never before in my life turned tail on anything and I spent a restless night pondering my action and wondering if I should have stayed, coped, proved myself once again and hoped for white approval. I shall never know.

The next day I was sent to a school just two days old. It was in utter contrast to the mausoleum from which I'd fled. It was a South London bungalow school with big windows, a landscaped playground and bright new paint everywhere.

Two women stood in the entrance hall chatting amicably. One was a determined-looking woman with a ruddy complexion and thick legs that looked like posts rising out of her shoes. The other, a soft-haired woman of about forty, seemed extremely calm in spite of the chaos that surged about her.

'Good morning,' I said to the fat-legged woman, 'are you the Headmistress?'

'No, this lady is.' She indicated her companion. The Head showed no reaction whatsoever to my colour, and if she had any doubts about my English, I could never have guessed. At once I felt welcome and she made me more so when she said, 'You're just in time to help us move in. We're in a mess, as you can see, but come into the staff-room and meet everybody.' As we approached the staff-room I could hear the sounds of lively chatter and the laughter of people who seemed to like being where they were. A short, good-looking, youngish man with an easy outgoing manner and honest eyes introduced himself as the Deputy Head. 'Have a cup of tea,' he said. 'How many lumps of sugar will you have? Most West Indians I know have three.' A suntanned girl in a plum-coloured jumper said in a thick Australian accent, 'I'm Gretta.' She offered me chocolates from a large box. Tea, sugar lumps and chocolate are anathema to me but I accepted all three and sat down.

Outside, dripping shrubs pressed close to the window and obscured the view, but the hands of the clock on the staff-room wall moved noiselessly past all my doubts and fears towards what must surely be a new and exciting life.

Minutes later a new bell rang and interrupted my thoughts. I hesitated. But the confident woman I'd met earlier in the entrance hall said, 'Come on. You're not the only one having kittens.' Before I could ask her what she meant she was away negotiating packets of books and piles of paper as if she was trudging through deep snow. My classroom was at the end of a clear, bright corridor and waiting for me was a crowd of mixed-age infants. They were mostly seven-year-olds with a sprinkling of six-year-olds. Some of the seven-year-olds looked big for their age and when I challenged them they insisted that they were seven, and then I remembered that English children are seven years old up to the very minute before their eighth birthday. With West Indian children the next milestone is always acknowledged and 'I'm six going on seven' is often heard.

Some of the children weren't sure whether or not they were in the right school and argued among themselves. The teachers of neighbouring schools, some said, had turned them out. Mothers who had rows with the teachers had sent us a few, and others who hated their old schools had come of their own accord. I was just thinking that the new school seemed to have attracted all the incorrigibles for miles around when a child said simply and honestly, 'I like new things. That's why I'm here.'

Alan, a boy big for his age who said his teacher had sent him to the new school, was well known to the children from the flats. A kind of awe came into their voices when they spoke to him. He was irascible and bullied those whom he considered the opposition with a thoroughness rooted in practice. He referred to his left fist as 'this' and to his right fist as 'that', and in no time had given himself the best chair, the best books, the best chalkboard, although they were all new. From time to time he shook his left fist, asked, "Oo wants this?' and tried to evict anyone who in his opinion shouldn't be in the school. At times, 'Take that!' would reach my ear and the thud of Alan's right fist would be followed by a whimper. I managed at last to calm them all and then sat down on one of their chairs to write their names in the new register. But at that moment the chair leg snapped beneath me and down I went. This was an unexpected gift to the class – the literal downfall of authority. The children laughed until they cried. Lynette, a perky auburn-haired child, offered me a helping hand but snatched it away again as part of the fun. And then I looked up and saw for good measure a whole row of mothers grinning through the glass. I waved bravely at them. If I knew anything about mothers, I had made their day. So much for a brand-new start. I picked myself up and set about restoring the situation. 'Since you're nearly all as big as I am,' I said, 'you'd better try your chairs and when you find a really strong one, sit on it.' The clusters of children broke up and bottoms gingerly made contact with chairs. It was all I could do to keep a straight face when I saw them lowering their tails as if the chairs were red-hot.

'Sit on your chairs when you're sure,' I encouraged them. And so at last we were off.

We were on the whole to get on well. I'd join them in the playground and watch them at play. This gave me many new insights into their personalities. I soon knew those who were part of groups and those who always stayed on the periphery. I knew those who had to bribe their way into play situations and those who were invited to play. I knew them all, the timid, the adventurous, the compulsive cheats and the ones who played by the rules. I noticed how they hid failure and how they coped with it and I learned to combine friendliness with firmness and so to bring a new understanding of discipline to my work.

In Guyana the teacher was expected to control her class and the class accepted this control. In school, children did not initiate, ask questions without permission, disobey or argue with the teacher. The teacher, it was assumed, knew all about education and how much should be dispensed and when. The teacher was expected to be knowledgeable about many things, and, if necessary, concerned enough about a child's progress to take steps to improve it. Every child who did not make progress in the school was an adverse comment upon the teacher.

She was a person to whom children and their parents would always be grateful. The child was not only respectful in her presence but if he was to be considered a good child he was obedient, passive, industrious and submissive. Children came to school wanting to learn. Teachers never taught by stealth as I now sometimes had to do.

This was the case with one little boy – the last in a big family. Brian was determined to do as little as possible at school. His favourite remarks were, 'Wot, readin' again?' or, 'Me do all that?' Although intelligent enough, he expected to be entertained at school. Meeting difficulties and coping with them weren't for him. He came in the morning scowling and frowning and greeted me with, 'I 'ate school. I 'ate 'aving to read and that.' His mother, who pushed him into the classroom and ran off to work, blamed the school for causing him to complain. She was always ready to blame teachers, and never associated words like 'love', 'friendship', 'respect' and 'understanding' with me.

Teachers, on the whole, were people who lived in a world which parents had once experienced and disliked intensely and now had no option but to let their children undergo the same experience. I was all right provided the children didn't complain. Some parents fussed to an incredible degree over what they described as their 'nippers', offering their breasts in a thousand and one disguises. Others had umbilical cords that stretched from home to school. These parents often came up to the school, and phrased any question in a way that immediately put me on the defensive, so that I began to imagine that I had infringed some code of behaviour that I knew nothing about.

Prejudice showed by innuendo and implication, and I reacted by overcompensation. My classroom became my obsession. I used it to prove to myself that I was once more the gifted teacher – the teacher who had been acclaimed in a far-away country. The thrusts of racial discrimination at that time were subtler than they are today but they were just as dispiriting. And so, after a time, I became disenchanted with teaching. Fear born of uncertainty and disorientation took hold of me. I no longer felt my work was valuable in the school society. At home, my job was teaching, as a chosen career – I had made a vital contribution to the literacy of underprivileged children. Now it had become a mere job of work and each day it was as if I was going into a boxing ring where any breach in the defence could put me flat on my back. I was one black among a gaggle of whites, depending on their approval, wondering about their sincerity, suspicious of any attempts to make a friend of me. I always had to think of the West Indians who were to come and be teachers in the future. I was a pioneer, an ambassador, and patronising words wounded me deeply, since all I wanted was to be left alone to do my job without feeling I was always being watched, assessed, measured and compared.

In those days there were determined attempts to keep black people out of Brixton, and some of the children went on weekend protest marches and came back to school to tell me all about it, and to express some of the sentiments they'd absorbed. David was one such child. One morning he produced the inevitable, 'You lived in a tree and you didn't wear no clothes till you come 'ere, didn't you?'

Parents and their prejudices were still at the roots of all the problems I met. Graeme's mother constantly criticised him.

If I agreed with her she turned on me. If I said nothing I was taking no interest in her kid.

It was bewildering to see how some parents used their children as mouthpieces to express their prejudices or, by putting words in their mouths, as vehicles to criticise what was being done in the classroom. Others used their children to relive their own 'barren years', and even to get attention. Sometimes I felt sorry for those mothers who appeared to have lost all sense of their identity, particularly when the last child was admitted to school. In their efforts to feel wanted they endlessly prinked the children outside my classroom door, or kissed them long and tenderly. One mother ceremoniously offered various bits of food, which the child, too perceptive to refuse, would slyly drop on the floor behind the coats.

The children made their own sense of what was done or said to them. I can recall Brian's puzzled face when he said, 'My mum takes a long time to kiss me goodbye and then she has to comb my hair again. I feel fed up.' Kim on the other hand made a most telling comment on the mouthings of the anti-immigrant community. 'If people keep Brixton white the flowers and the trees will have to be white as well, won't they, and I won't be able to see them.'

Sometimes their comments took a more humorous turn. Shula, whose mum thought her a cut above the others, talked endlessly of their au pair girl.

'What's an au pair girl?' I said, in the interest of their general knowledge. Robert's face lit up. 'I know,' he said. 'It's fings wot people can have. My dad wants to have one, but my mum won't let him have one.' Concealing my smile, I commended the clarity and confidence with which he spoke.

Some of the children had a charming innocence and talked fearlessly of their experiences. In this way I sensed their needs and tried to cater for them in my classroom.

The flats from which most of them came confined their ideas of beauty, space and reality, and in their childish imagination and thinking set limits to what was possible from day to day.

I realised that I should aim to make all my contacts with the children viable and try to touch them in ways that they had not experienced before. I turned to art and drama to help them towards an awareness of alternatives and to set new boundaries in their thinking. By watching them act out all kinds of situations I gained insights into their understanding of right and wrong, of fairness and unfairness, and of the way they dealt with domestic situations of all sorts.

'Miss,' said Rachelle one day when they were playing 'Clinics', 'how do you spell "contraceptive pills"? I want this baby to have them.'

'Give the baby some Disprin,' I said, 'that would do just as well.' I was dying to explain but fear of her mum accusing me of telling her dirty things prevented me. By helping the children to clarify their ideas, I was able to clarify my own.

Their world of work and the part they must play in it was sharply divided and I was able to test its character, its flavour and the meaning it held for each child.

I asked them to draw and talk about the people they saw at work in the community and to describe their feelings about different kinds of work. The 'when I grow up' sessions we held showed that the fireman, the train driver, the postman and the mounted police were the most popular workers.

Sometimes, wearing a simple prop such as a label, a hat or a mask, the children acted out the roles of their favourite workers, drawing on dialogue and gesture when 'school-talk' failed them. The children whose parents did what we called the 'handy jobs' heard their work being discussed with respect and some became confident enough to bring additional information. Janet, whose father was a milkman, told us the reason why milk-bottle tops varied in colour. Susan brought instructions on how to decorate a room written out in a clear neat hand. Pat, who at first hid when the others said her father was a coalman, brought us some fine samples of coal when interest made her courageous enough to do so, and Paul, the greengrocer's son, brought us pictures of English apples with prices attached. All this helped to give the children the chance to form new precepts, opinions and judgements about situations, incidents and people.

Through the use of the excellent school library, and a 'Work Interest Corner', which was kept going with information supplied by parents, the children were given the opportunity to extend their experiences.

The generous display areas in the school encouraged experiment with graphic materials. The children painted in order to experience and explore. When they painted my house they painted flats, sometimes with trees beside them for me to climb.

My food was a different matter. There were plates full of people for me to eat. Some were ordinary people fully clad, others were stick people, very frail and delicate, with salt, pepper and tomato ketchup beside them.

The children painted out their doubts and their inhibitions. One day Alan showed me his painting – a group of grotesque people praising an object which he described as 'they God'. There was a solitary black figure in the background.

'Why is that one black?' I asked, expecting to be told that it was the Devil.

'That's you seeing that they behave theirself,' he said seriously.

Through the use of materials of all kinds I could find out how the children were affected by the discipline which each kind of material brought. To some children materials were not to be handled with care if they belonged to someone else. To others some kinds of materials, like clay, plasticine or papier-mâché, were considered dirty or messy. To some they held magic, and gave delight and a sense of achievement, which encouraged the children to reach out for new goals and to adjust to others. But it was still hard to be comfortable with those who stayed in the shadows of the activities I provided. These were in particular the hyperactive, the hostile, or the timid children. Living as I did in the country of my skin, all the methods I used had to be acceptable to white observers.

Bruce came into my class as tense as can be. He asked my permission before he attempted the smallest thing, and sought my approval at every turn. His mother tapped me on the shoulder one day and said, 'Ay, you know he don't like black, don't you? It's a serious colour. Very, very serious. They was all wearing it when his grandad died. Loved his grandad, he did.'

Day after day, Bruce gave the impression of rigid control and fear of criticism. He was unable to improvise or enjoy anything we did.

'What do you like doing best?' I asked.

After a lot of 'dunnos', he said, 'Ea'in' fruit like pears and thingys.'

So we made a beautiful frieze of fruits cut out in black and mounted on a white background. Bruce arranged the fruits very tastefully indeed and we hung it in the hall. Everyone admired it.

'Black's not such a bad colour after all,' I said.

'I know,' he replied, 'only my mum keeps on saying that it is.'

Music helped the children to live out their fantasies. I linked the music to stories and went to great lengths to choose records which would extend rhythmic limits and help social integration as well. Linda, who came from a family notorious round the flats for fecklessness and irresponsibility of all sorts, met with hostility in the classroom. Approach to the group was quite beyond her capacities. She had no energy to initiate and lacked the ability to sustain group contacts. No one wanted to hold her hand or share a place with her. During music, when she became a part of the group experience, she was accepted, and as she felt less threatened, she relaxed. Terry, on the other hand, was an aggressive, hostile child who used the nails from the woodwork box to communicate the tensions he built up in a confining relationship with his mother. He had been a premature baby and this in the eyes of his mother labelled him an invalid for life. So deep were his feelings of hate and hostility to women in authority that his eyes became almost blood-red when he was angry. He accepted nothing except what went on in his own little pin-head, spoke rudely to everyone and used nails with creative sadism. Music became a challenge to him to monitor his own emotions, control his own movements and test his own ideas, and by acting as an integrating agent calmed him and opened the way to constructive relationships. His steps became lighter when he danced and his eyes softened. He later stopped the arguments in which he so delighted and learned to play and share. He was even able to 'fall in love' with one of the nice girls before his seventh birthday.

The materials the children used gave an insight into their vocabularies and made them dredge up experiences. They were encouraged to describe what they did accurately and gave instructions which I would record for other children to follow.

'I got this eggshell, see,' said Terry after he'd stopped hurting people, 'and I scrump it up and mixed it with some paste and put it all the way round, right away round the thing what I drawed.'

When I asked the class who knew how to 'scrump', Terry laughed until he cried.

Sometimes their words went a little awry, as when Dennis walked around the class looking to see which one of us had flexible legs. He really loved that word and wrote stories about the lady who had flexible legs.

They learned never to be afraid of words, however long or strange they were. Through 'Art with Words' they developed ideas of taste, style and beauty and found language to describe them. They got a feeling of accomplishment. They learned to relax and to laugh. They developed protective attitudes like caring and being concerned with others, and came to know what ownership of a prized possession meant. And because of this I was able to take things such as my miniature porcelain animals, my piece of Christolian glass and other things which were important to me for them to share with me. They knew I valued my things for one reason alone – because quite early I had learned the difference between the shoddy and the cheap – the ugly and the beautiful.

Suddenly I realised that my role as a teacher had changed. From being the dominant character in the learning situation I was now a partner, concerned not only with outcomes and aims but with attitudes, pace of learning, and individual differences in children. No longer were they a class, but individuals with patterns of thinking, perceptions, and imagination different not only from those of their peers but different indeed from my own.

Once again teaching began to excite me and while I was in the grip of this new excitement we were told to prepare for what was to be a challenging experience – for me. This was the Open Day or the one day a year on which the parents officially visited the school.

Staff varied in their attitudes to Open Day. The general attitude was one of resignation and a desire to make the best of it. I was not too keen on contact with the parents *en masse*. But I knew my class well enough to anticipate the reactions I would meet. I was a rarity in those days and that could work for or against me, depending on the level of intolerance. I displayed each child's work regardless of parental status and without making any assumptions about whether the parents would attend or not. School is a formal place, calling for formal language and acceptable social behaviour, and many parents dislike this. With but a few exceptions, the attendance was good and when the parents saw the children's interaction with me they appeared to think my efforts were worthwhile. They were unconcerned with abstractions and were mainly interested in their own children's progress in the three Rs. The more opinionated among them assumed that if our teaching was effective the children would learn, but no one attempted to question the methods we used. It amused me to see the way some parents took their children's abilities for granted. If they were good at their job they expected their children to be good at school, since as far as they could see the same set of skills was involved.

I was by now especially interested in those children with learning difficulties. From observing them I felt that however much the environment tantalised them, these children were inhibited by something within themselves from going joyfully towards learning. I tried to link what I did at school to what they could do at home with little help from parents, siblings or friends. Slowly I built up in these children a need to achieve. I picked out something worthwhile in whatever they did, and worked through their feelings about themselves, their school, their teachers and anything else which bore on their lives. We used the television programmes, the billboards, the Pools and papers with which many of them were familiar for reading, art and discussion, and slowly attitudes changed for the better. The children who were slow learners realised that they could make particular contributions to class life, and lost their self-consciousness. I encouraged them to describe themselves to me, to notice what they wore to school each day – to become aware of what went on round about them. They talked about everything.

Louise said, 'My mum doesn't like thunder. When it comes she goes under the stairs.'

James, who always crept up on me and had difficulty settling down, said, 'My dad sleeps all day. I have to creep about at home.' After that I stopped glaring at him when he made me jump.

The subjects were many and varied. 'My cat had five kittens. We had to put some of their heads in water. I don't want to go to the Baths no more.'

'Someone broke into our house and stole our money. At nights I dream that they come back to kill us.'

'When I went to see the New Forest, a rabbit got killed. Its blood was on our car. "Wash it off," said my dad. "It's paint."'

'My grandad gave me a pound and my mum gave me a pound and I bought a big teddy. Now we don't know where to put it. We only have one room.'

'I went to a wedding and I danced and my dad danced with my mum and I and Grandad danced and we all danced in our new shoes and our new clothes and our new coats.'

The pace, the temperature and the pulse of the classroom had to suit each child. If the classroom was too stimulating, and offered too many choices, if it made demands upon the children which to them seemed meaningless, or set goals which were to them remote, they became bored, unsettled and unco-operative. Some children came to school with a deep sense of failure. I was often told, 'My mum says I can't do anything. She has to do it for me.' Such children expected me to take Mum's place and it was no use rejecting the role. Together we divided the work into pieces and we each did some. Later the children were coaxed into taking over the whole task.

Motivating them all, reassuring them, building up channels of communication and feelings in the classroom was an enormous task but by breaking new ground, different patterns of thinking and new ideas sprouted in my mind.

Once a week I forgot about school and re-entered the world of the Commonwealth student, although strictly speaking I no longer belonged to it.

Beryl at a supper dance at the University of London
with her fellow students, 1954

The world of the young Commonwealth immigrant of the early fifties was full of political talk. People slept, dreamt and lived politics. The federation of the Rhodesias, the independence of the Gold Coast, and British exploitation of the colonies were burned into our throats. We were all going to put this world to rights in five or six moves.

The left-wing students wooed us with offers of cheap digs, and promises of supplementary rations, but any kind of overture from white students was bound to be suspect. This suspicion had been set over the centuries and it would take oceans of water to wash away such deep conditioning. It was our first contact with whites on a wide uncensored front of relationships and although there was never any love lost between them, the Africans and the West Indians usually followed the same line in their dealings with white people. We were amused by some of it, especially their affairs with white women, whose naivety was really quite extraordinary. These girls believed, by and large, that at the end of the chase after a black man lay a bigger and better orgasm. Many of the men professed that they were only paying back in kind what generations of black women suffered over the centuries in silence and degradation. Here there was naivety too, since in our part of the world people of all races married and lived in bliss and harmony till death. When I was with the children all consciousness of race and colour, white hatred of blacks and black bewilderment over white arrogance receded, since these came at all times out of the hearts and minds of the adults who surrounded the children. To them I was their teacher – someone who treated them fairly even if at times firmly, who worked hard to help them, and to whom they could turn for help and comfort and sympathy.

But I wanted more responsibility, and began to examine my position as a teacher. As far as I could see into the future I would always be at the bottom of the hierarchy. It would have been useless to apply for a post which depended on an interview. In fact I wouldn't even have been called for interview. The Local Authority for which I worked was enlightened and would have presented no difficulty but then there were the managers, the inspectors and the Headteachers themselves. My knowledge of the system was not 'inbred', I was told. Whatever I did, however effectively I taught, someone somewhere wouldn't have been convinced that I was able to do more. It was very depressing to me to be forced by colour to accept the status quo, especially when I saw colleagues much less qualified seeking and getting promotion.

I enrolled for further evening study, which involved working in the university library. One Saturday as I waited for a girlfriend to show up I noticed a young Englishman eyeing me. I suppose he was amused by my display of impatience and after I'd asked him the time, we got talking. It was as if I'd known him all my life. When my friend at last arrived I was sorry to leave him but he said, 'See you next week,' as if we had been meeting there all our lives.

When next we met we talked about everything under the sun and it was the first time in my life that I had met a man to whom I could look up. His mind fascinated me and very soon I could count him among my friends. My experience with him and his family was different from any I had had before. 'Does the fact that I'm a spade worry you?' I asked him in the language of the time, and his reply, 'I am looking for quality of a certain kind. Where I find it, nothing else matters,' clinched our relationship from that moment. We walked and talked and spent many pleasant hours together and then one day we decided to get married, and did so without much fuss. Our marriage concerned us two and the rest of the world didn't matter because we weren't prepared to let it. His love for me was based on respect: respect for me as a person in my own right, respect for my mind, my sensibilities and my integrity. Subconsciously, I suppose I saw him as a buffer between this society and myself and as someone who could interpret its subtle nuances for me.

Whatever my reasons, it was a happy time for me. I had

settled for nest-building with all the attendant difficulties which a mixed marriage could bring in this blood- and lineage-conscious country. But we were prepared to build a future together with its basis in mutual respect, friendly awareness, trust and affection.

Strangely, my marriage caused the children's mothers to warm towards me. At last before their eyes, something had happened to me which they could understand. I had gone steady, got married and with luck would have a few kids. They were seeing me for the first time in relation to themselves and probably hoped that I would better understand the fabric and the foundations of their lives.

I had become an individual in my own right, able to make effective decisions. No more common-room politics for me, no more frenzied jiving with the crowd. I could now concern myself with the other more meaningful things of life.

After much difficulty we found a flat and with relief I stood by the window pinching myself to make sure it was real. By sheer chance, I looked up and saw the most beautiful sunset that I'd ever seen. It stayed long enough to show me that colours could fuse magically and with a glory all their own, and the result of that fusion could give the feeling of pure delight.

The children played at weddings with abandon. They collected pictures of brides and grooms from the local papers and we made a wedding book. The interest ran into dozens of other activities. We even had a magic car which ran off with the important guests at the doll's wedding. There were echoes of *Toytown* in the sequence but we had masses of fun.

Furnishing my flat involved them too. We made a plan of the flat, and they listed the furniture which I ought to have.

They fell about laughing whenever I said 'suite' in relation to furniture. They collected strange names and I can well remember the amusement that words like 'chest of drawers', 'gate-leg table', 'sideboard' and 'easy-chair' caused. The old junk shops in the area provided new interest and Neil, whose mother knew something about Victorian furniture, drew a 'what-not', an ottoman and a 'dinner waggon' for us.

However, the children's interest switched dramatically when Stephen's budgie died and had to be buried. The stories of dead pets came thick and fast and the games took on a more sombre note.

Just at this point, I was given the first half-coloured child I ever taught. She had been adopted by some people in the flats. Her mother was lovely with her but went out of her way to say that the girl was adopted. This made her 'out group' on two counts: being adopted was like having an incurable disease; she was also what the children described as an 'arf-caste' and they took delight in tormenting her. Alan told me of the family 'up Kentish Town' whom his brothers and he persecuted. I felt sorry for little coffee-coloured Patricia and protected her, but this was the worst step I could have taken, and I soon realised that eventually her ability to fight her own battles would help her to establish her identity in the group. She cried when they called her 'blackie' and then one day she plucked up her courage and accused Alan of 'not knowing what black looks like'. Names like Chocolate Drop and Gum Drop went back and forth until I said that it would be much better if they wrote out their insults. I provided a box for the slips and once a week read them out as they were written. The children thought it hilarious when I read:

Shuklit Drip (Chocolate Drop)
Gum Drup (Gum Drop)
Kol face (Coal Face)
Spads (Spades)
Whit fac (White Face)
    and
Bluckies (Blackies).

Since their repertoire of names was limited, the game soon starved itself to death.

Then Lola, an African child who had been fostered with whites, was admitted. Her foster-mother dressed her impeccably in colours that emphasised the blackness, which obsessed them all. Lola wanted to be like everyone else and my attempts to identify with her only made her more distraught. She had been given a colour problem long before she came to school, and felt extremely sorry for herself. She buried our black doll in the sand, and ill-treated it whenever she could. She always sought the best for herself and when she wasn't petulant she was sulky. Patricia was given a better deal after Lola arrived and joined in whole-heartedly when the other children teased Lola. Then one day things changed. Roger announced that he was going to marry Lola when they grew up. 'I told my mum,' he said, 'and she said wait and see.' He and Lola played and she seemed happier.

'Why will you marry Lola?' I asked. 'It's a long time before you grow up.'

'Well, when we play horses, she runs very fast indeed. And that would be nice,' he said.

The children always had reasons for doing things very different from mine. But Lola now had a friend who liked her and with whom she played. Roger was always her partner and always sat with her and shared with her. She no longer had deep feelings of rejection. She shared everything with him and by doing so learned to share with others. Some of the affection the class had for Roger was shown to her and all her actions became positive and pleasing.

A few months later I became pregnant and decided to leave the school. I told the children about the baby and although they could see me getting fatter they asked no questions. They believed that the stork brought some babies, others could be found under the gooseberry bushes and when the weather was too cold for that one bought babies at the hospital. Even worldly-wise Alan made no other statement except that I would one day have a baby. They all brought their cast-off toys for me to keep till the baby arrived and one of the first Greek girls I ever taught brought a Christmas card prematurely addressed to Mrs Baby esq. They brought me cuttings of babies from women's magazines but could not imagine that my baby wouldn't be quite like them. I encouraged them to bring pictures of themselves as babies, pinned them up and gave tiny coloured buttons to the winners of our 'Guess the Baby' competition.

But at last the time came when I was expected to leave. 'I'll always give you a post here,' said the Headmistress. In her I'd seen a quiet, dedicated interest in children at work and it was nice to be leaving on such a note. In her school I had learned how to help children gather their experiences into an orderly system which they could call upon in future, and to look more closely at the needs of individual children. I learned to assess the value or otherwise of an environment that was constantly changing. Teaching, I now knew, was a science, which called for the skilful use of aids. Compared with mothers at home, mothers in this country spent much more time with their children and this had to be considered when children were expected to adapt to a school where they might be taught by a teacher who is not physically 'like Mummy'.

But most important of all, I'd learned that to succeed as a black teacher, an immigrant had to be twice as good as everyone else.

My little nest beckoned to me and, with few regrets, I took the road to motherhood. There would be no interference from family – no dependence on those baby books that tell mothers how to cope. I felt confident and hopeful. I was sure life held many golden moments for me.

9

'You're a mum, now'

I hadn't been home for long before I discovered that although I might well be a natural 'nester', I wasn't really cut out for nest-building itself. Chores came hard to me and so I tackled them with all the more determination. The very thought that neighbours might visit and find a speck of dirt mortified me. Actually, no one ever came.

Nevertheless, with total fanaticism, I kept up my labours, and was to do so during all the years of devoted motherhood. I had to be the perfect housewife and perfect mother. I must be above all possible white criticism.

I worried, too, about my child to be – the product of what was called 'miscegenation'. It wasn't its colour or the texture of its hair that bothered me, but its wholeness. Might there not be some flaw in the chromosomes? Again, the society in which I now lived had conditioned my way of thinking.

Reading didn't help. The libraries were full of books about mulattos, most of whom seemed to have been notorious for one reason or another. After I had defeated an army of nightmares my fears subsided, but I remember to this day the anxiety with which I first examined my son, seeking some flaw, born of a fear buried deep down inside me.

The children had kept in touch all the time through letters and cards and so when the baby came we went to visit them.

They crowded round us in the playground.

'You still a teacher?' asked Susan.

'Of course,' I replied.

'Can't be,' Susan persisted. She couldn't see how I could play two parts at once. 'You're a mum, now. You got a baby.'

'You gonna beat 'im now and then?' asked Alan. ''Ere, you can 'ave my belt.' He whipped it off and handed it to me.

My son was now asleep in my arms.

'Look at 'im 'avin' 'is kip!' drooled Gloria. 'Lovely, ain't 'e. What's 'is name?'

'Paul,' I said.

'Me brother's name is Paul,' said Gloria.

'An' me friend's name is Paul,' said Susan.

'Park 'im for a bit, Miss,' pleaded Alan, bored by now with babies. 'Come along and play with us.'

So I 'parked' him with a school helper and went along with them to play with them.

The next week we moved into suburbia.

We moved into what I always think of as a sort of twilight country, indeterminate between sleeping and waking, muted and barely alive. We were observed from behind the curtains. For weeks no one smiled or talked to us. They mustn't be seen by the neighbours talking to a black woman or a bearded white man.

'Would these people's faces crack if they tried a smile?' I asked myself. 'Would their heads drop off if they gave a nod? Would their tongues catch fire if they passed the time of day?' They all seemed so sad.

Soon some came hawking their wares. God was frequently offered. I couldn't really see why. Did I look as if I needed Him more than anyone else? No matter. They hawked God with everything – tracts, cards, magazines, books, pictures and pamphlets.

A wishy-washy little lady in a neat beige coat and well-worn felt hat came frequently. At the most unlikely moments she would knock. 'Hello, again. Come to see you!' She was sure she had a special offer. After a few trite words about the state of the world, she would launch into her big production number – the state of my soul.

'Do you believe in God?'

On one occasion she added, 'Do you know what the Devil is like, is really like?'

Since I was busy with other matters I replied, 'Of course I do. He's prancing about in my heart right now and he's telling me to pour a bucket of cold water over you and chase you out.'

She changed her tune, dumping the Devil. 'Oh, why not let us pray together?' she appealed.

In my country it is sacrilege to refuse prayer. But I wasn't in my country – I was somewhere else.

'You must be barmy,' I replied. 'After I've bathed the baby, seen to his nappies and scrubbed the kitchen I'll follow you all the way to Mecca, if you like – but not now.'

Since she still lingered, I suggested, 'If you want to be of some help lend a hand with the nappies. The Nappy Service man calls about ten.'

My son was a healthy chap, thoroughly breastfed, and he did justice to his nappies. She took one look at the pile, straightened her hat and rushed out.

When it wasn't God, it was rubbish they hawked – all kinds of rubbish.

There was one caller who had plainly missed her vocation.

She was a hustler, although her tightly encased bust, her speck-led arms and generous hips made her look more like an all-in wrestler.

Her teeth, stained with tobacco, had a pink over-wash from her lipstick. She flicked her cigarette ash indiscriminately. The make-up line on a face plastered with cream was as definite as any road sign.

'Getting on all right?' she asked at our first meeting. 'Takes time, don't it?'

She tried to smile with her eyes but only succeeded in dis-lodging an eyelash.

'Got some clothes,' she said. 'Belong to a friend of mine. Bargains they are. Just your size – four pounds the lot. I'll take ten bob a week.'

'No, thank you,' I said, 'I've got loads of clothes. Besides, I make my own.'

'Oh, but you can't make 'em like this,' she insisted. 'You can't make quality. Feel! They're samples, you see. My cousin – I mean my friend – always buys samples.'

'No, thank you,' I said.

She stroked her chin for a moment with a manicured anger and then suddenly her generosity soared as if on wings.

'Tell you what,' she said, 'I'll give 'em to you. Take 'em all, I feel charitable.'

'The rag-and-bone man will be glad of them,' I said. 'I don't want them.'

She left abruptly and I felt relieved but the next morning there was a large bag of old clothes on the steps. I threw them in the dustbin.

'D'you like the clothes?' she asked when next I met her.

I told her what I'd done with them.

'But black people like old clothes,' she said forcefully. 'Everyone knows that.'

'Black people don't like old clothes,' I corrected. 'And everyone, it seems, does not know that.'

But it didn't stop her coming. She came frequently with old curtains, odds and ends of cutlery, odd cups and saucers – anything she didn't want. It was as if she were suffering from some compulsion to sell me things. And, for my part, I was just as determined that I would never buy them.

I got the impression that what bothered her was that I wasn't conforming to some mythical pattern.

One day she asked in desperation, 'Why aren't you black in your ways?'

'I am,' I said, 'only you can't see that I am.'

Making sense of people's attitudes was now the main difficulty in my life. Ignorance was rife. One day I took my son to the welfare clinic, and was forced by the delay in seeing the doctor to feed him there.

My brown breast with the darker circle around the nipple was a major attraction to the woman who sat beside me. 'Look at it!' she appealed to all the other mothers, 'that blackness round 'er tits! D'you reckon that's good for the baby?'

I could cheerfully have hit her.

But the health visitor pounced on her at once. 'Oh, don't be daft!' she said. 'Look at him. He's lovely. You can see that he gets everything that's good for him. Look at his nappies – sparkling white.'

That did mean something to them. 'Yeh, whiter than white,' the woman whispered hoarsely.

It was almost a religious concept – whiter than white.

'Yeh,' they all breathed devoutly – a sort of suburban Greek chorus – 'whiter than white!'

It wasn't always like that – especially with Sylvie and Ricky. While they were waiting for their own house to be built they'd moved into one of the luxury flats next door. Ricky had made his 'pile' selling scrap metal after the war and was spending it extravagantly on Sylvie. She in turn was very indulgent to their child, a very blonde baby with a big head.

Sylvie had no qualms whatsoever about inviting me to call. 'Come and have a nosh!' she'd say over the telephone.

And what a nosh it always turned out to be! Tea, toast, pastries, cream cakes and fruit – with the big-headed baby having a taste of absolutely everything. ''Ere you are, love, 'ave a lick of this,' or, ''Ave a suck at that.'

Ricky's favourite retort was, 'Buy it.' 'You want it, doll,' he would say to Sylvie, 'you buy it!'

High upon Sylvie's shopping list was the brand-new nose she was going to have. She would spend hours drawing it. Then she would be seized by uncertainty and solicit her husband's help.

'Which one, Rick?' she'd say. 'Now look at me drawings. Which one d'you reckon? You choose the best.'

And he'd console her. 'It don't matter, doll. You 'ave any one you like. Buy it! Buy the plastic surgeon an' all. Buy the 'ospital! Buy the bleedin' lot!'

They loved to be read to – rather in the way that children like a regular story. I read Somerset Maugham's *Rain* to Sylvie and she sat there transfixed.

Then she said, quite suddenly, 'Why don't you learn me to

read like you, Beryl, so that I can surprise my mum? She's ever such a good reader.'

I agreed and without more ado Sylvie fished out some Blackberry Farm books which she'd bought for the baby 'to chew on' and decided that she'd read those. They were not the books I would have chosen for an adult learner but we began.

'Read all the words you know,' I said. She laboured over the few words she knew, making all the usual learner's mistakes, and I could see that her attitude to reading would have to be changed. Reading calls for application, involvement, concentration and discipline, and these Sylvie regarded as posh.

As soon as she grew tired of handling her disability, she played games with me – all the naughty schoolgirl games she had played with her teachers when she was a little girl and failing at reading. This time, however, her partner in crime was her 'little innocent' rather than one of her mates, and she could break any rule, real or imagined, while wiggling round in her diaphanous nightie, or brushing her hair with a silver-backed art nouveau brush, or pouring expensive scent down her cleavage.

She expected me to give her up as she so often said her teacher had done. But I disappointed her by suggesting that we wrote some letters to Ricky so that she could read them to him while they sipped their sherry 'of an evening'. To get her confidence I had to use some of the phrases and words she used. She struggled to get the words to describe her actions accurately and drawing on her repertoire of popular songs we managed to put together the first letter. I was amazed at the amount of repetition one could get by just stringing the titles of songs together. And with all the pride she could muster over anything not directly concerned with the baby, she read: 'Ricky, my darling, you are my one true love, my only love. When you look at me I see stars in your eyes. Tell me that you are here today to stay with me for ever and ever.' Sylvie smiled broadly and said, 'Cods, it is. A load of cods! But I like it.'

She brought out all the groceries from her cupboard and while manicuring her nails tried to read the labels on them. She was still learning to read when they moved away several months later. If she gave up the difficult struggle then perhaps the Adult Literacy Scheme will encourage her to have another try.

Close by lived a woman who was to become a very real friend. Her face had been hideously burned in the war and at first sight it made an awful impact. We met in the local park and from then on we'd often share a bench and talk.

Somehow she could still radiate goodwill and good cheer. Somehow she could still make a joke of misfortune. When people stared at us she'd ask, 'Is it you or me?'

'Your colour's like my face,' she once said. 'We've both got physical defects. Come to think of it, I'd rather be black any day.'

A point came when I seemed to have been overtaken by a kind of illness, born of isolation and loss of identity. I began to need my own kind. In the street I would begin looking into black faces, hoping that in some black face or other I would find some satisfaction of an intense psychological need.

I shall never forget how I found it . . .

I now had a baby daughter, Darla-Jane, and I'd taken her with me to meet my husband. As I parked the pram outside, a well-built, elderly West Indian woman stood watching me. She worked, I guessed, in the private nursing home nearby.

She smiled the warm smile of kinship that I'd been seeking and yet my reaction was different from what I expected. Here was a black face that promised something, and yet suspicion, not gratitude, came over me.

'Good afternoon, dear,' she said. 'This is your baby?' The odd thing was that her accent seemed to make her a complete stranger. It really was ages since I'd heard a West Indian accent besides my own.

'Why 'er so clear? Your husband a white man?'

'No, an Eskimo,' I said indifferently.

'Never hear 'bout them,' she replied pleasantly, 'but they must be white people, too.'

'No, just Eskimoes,' I said again.

Suddenly she touched my arm with a finger as if to find a spot for an injection.

'Teach your baby to love black,' she counselled. 'Is a hard colour to love. Tell 'er from me black is the colour of life, not death. The world was black in its own morning time. Eskimo or not – learn 'er how to love black.'

And then she added, 'Learn 'er, too, to love everyone black or white, 'cause no one is really sure about the colour of God.'

At that moment she became real to me. I had forgotten that kind of West Indian – the West Indian of infinite wisdom, who mixed curiosity with kinship, who seemed always to walk with God.

I pointed through the library door. 'My husband', I said, 'is the man handing in books at the counter.'

'Oh, oh,' she said, 'he looks as if he has a big heart.'

The way she spoke gave my feeling for my family just the impetus it needed. Our meeting, brief though it was, proved a turning-point. It was as if, all at once, the discords had gone and left only the purest notes of love and commitment. Suddenly all my fears fell away.

I knew I had to be happy in spite of the assumptions that were made about blacks. It wasn't easy to tell the wise from the stupid, the bigots from those who genuinely sought information. Quite consciously I closed the dichotomy in my heart. No longer must there be a side where the whites lived with their words and their weapons and a black side where we lived with our wounds and our medicaments.

I realised that my husband had become completely buried in the shifting sands of my emotions. He'd never complained but now quite suddenly it was all different. It was no longer for me essentially a marriage of true minds. All of a sudden there he was – alone in my heart.

Now I was free to enjoy the grass and the sky and the birdsong. Even the mud-grey water in the pond in our park seemed beautiful. I enjoyed my children. I did my best to keep their perceptions of people and their actions clear and clean. I offered to help people. I offered especially to help people with young children. It didn't matter if they declined. Life was easier now.

We lived in a part of London peopled mainly by well-to-do business and professional men and their families. They bought their children expensive toys and naturally enough my children wanted bicycles like their friends and the loss of my income made a noticeable difference. So I looked about for ways in which I could earn some extra money. My experience in teaching reading could be useful but I was reluctant to work through an agency as a straight remedial teacher. I have always had individual ideas about remedial work so I decided to offer a private specialised service which would live up to the high expectations of the local parents.

I knew from past experience that a child's conflict with himself, his family or with school invariably showed itself in his reading ability, and so I offered to help those children whose reading performance was inadequate by approaching the problem from a number of different angles. The course I started included painting, active reading games which brought in word recognition and phonics, body awareness, music, listening games, being read to and then reading for themselves – in that order.

It would have been easy just to concentrate on the mistakes the children made, and to analyse and treat them. But these were intelligent children who had become past masters at hiding their failure to read and at avoiding anything else directly connected with it. Clowning, precocity, cheek, showing off, barefaced rudeness and imaginary illnesses were all part of the ploy.

We began the programme by talking. The children were discouraged from using such phrases as 'my mum says' or 'my dad thinks' except when they were expressing their own ideas, stating their interests or describing and interpreting their experiences. The children talked about themselves, about what made them laugh or cry, frightened or delighted them or made them jealous, and discussed their likes and dislikes. The active games we played made them unselfconscious enough to discuss their emotions. They became people in their own right, able to break out of the straitjacket of parental dreams and expectations in which they were held. I helped them to build up their own expectancies, to think of the interests and excitements of each new day. Finding new interests, they came to terms with their inability to read and felt less ashamed of it.

Some of the children had difficulty in adjusting to the demands of school, its discipline and its differences from home life, and simply opted out. Parents hardly ever realised that children were no more in control of their achievement at school than babies are of their bowel movement. My experience with children had taught me that it was encouragement, security, certainty of love and full confidence in a relationship which motivated a child.

The children came expecting to be bored. They looked for the dreaded reading books and expected to be criticised, corrected and pushed beyond their capacity. Instead I read poems and beautiful passages of prose by writers such as Kenneth Grahame, Oscar Wilde, Rumer Godden and many others. When eventually I heard them read we joked about the difficult words they'd meet, and drew funny shapes around them, which fixed them in the child's mind and cut down the expectation of failing and the sense of failure. They found the will to cope and wanted to read. It had become a challenge.

I also had sessions with the parents during which I explained the complex nature of the reading process, the importance of choosing the right books, and the parents' role in helping a child to cope with his difficulties.

So successful was my class that the children learned to read and stopped coming. I then started doing freelance journalism and some broadcasting, but I felt I wanted more social involvement so I started a mothers' club for mothers with young children. We met once a week for a couple of hours and discussed anything that interested us – the children, books, films and plays, women's magazines, food, the local schools. The question of colour didn't arise; our relationship was based on similarity of intellect and matching interests.

When discussing schools I offered the suggestion that school consciousness should start with maternity classes. A school should be a focal point in the community and children should have access to it from their earliest days so that the stress that was often associated with it by children could be prevented. Children, I said, should first see their teachers as people, then as friends, and finally as teachers. I urged them to remember the significant relationships of their own childhood and to try to recall how they were affected by them, and also to try to find the source of any inadequacy they might have and decide how to prevent its being repeated in their children.

But still, despite these rewarding exchanges, there were bad moments. Our fruit trees were laden but my pears were unacceptable to some local people. The waifs who lived in the Council Home, however, had no such scruples. It was through my gifts of fruit to them that I walked into a happening so totally surprising in every aspect that it proved to me finally that life can always make a fool out of fiction.

The Council Home had been greeted by a predictable howl in the local paper. Nobody had mentioned colour – only social attitudes, habits and classes. But the fact was there for everyone to see – a good sprinkling of coloured or foreign faces among the children who spilt out of the Home every morning on their way to the local school. It was a time when immigrants were pouring into the country to beat the Act of Parliament intended to curb the flow.

Houses would be devalued. The children would leave a trail

of damage. So went the arguments on the Letters page. Actually the children were rather self-contained and over-timid. I'd befriended one in particular, a little girl called Lesley, whom I'd found crying regularly – always by the same pillar-box.

I'd gone along to the Home, familiar to me now through friendships made by apples and pears, to ask the Warden if Lesley could come to tea. My son, now five years old, was with me to support the invitation.

And then, just as I was turning the corner near the Home, I heard a loud greeting, 'Nye!'

Nye? Several bells were set ringing for me, and the most insistent wasn't the one summoning to mind the Rt Hon. Member for Ebbw Vale. No, I thought more especially about a baby who'd been dumped in another Home.

We turned the corner and on the steps of this Home I saw a man talking to a tall and well-built boy. There was something worryingly familiar about the man. He was neatly dressed but looked worn and tired. He was carrying a bumpy, brown paper bag.

Then it clicked. Good heavens! Delroy.

'Delroy!' I shouted.

He turned, looking genuinely shocked, as well he might, at this reappearance of a witness of his not too salubrious past.

'What are you doing here?' I asked, and now he perked up and shook hands vigorously.

'My boy live in here, man,' he explained. 'You live round here?'

'With my family,' I replied. 'I have two now – a pair.'

Delroy chuckled. 'Look how times does fly, eh?' He put a hand on Nye's shoulder. 'He's eleven going on twelve now.' He held up the paper bag. 'He ask me to bring these bulbs, man. He doing gardening. But he won't see them turn to daffodils because we going back by Christmas.'

Nye nudged him and whispered.

Delroy laughed again, with an explanation. 'Great chap, Nye. He want half a crown. Always like money. He always like the filthy lucre when he see me.'

'You're really going home then, Delroy?' I asked.

'Yeh, thank God we're going home to Trinidad. He got plenty of relatives. He going to be all right. I been inside, man. I don't want that for him.'

We talked for a while but it wasn't easy with two restless boys in attendance and with Delroy caught in a mixture of moods. He was genuinely happy about going back home, perhaps just a little happy at seeing someone from the past. I thought he'd become much more serious than he was in that far-off time. Perhaps the future would be bright for poor Nye after all.

10

'She ain't got no spear'

During the period when I was cut off from teaching I still felt an urgent need to hear the sound of children at work and at play. I couldn't go past a school playground without stopping, listening and watching.

Children got to know me. They came to the fence and talked to me. They were mostly polite and friendly. They'd ask me for stamps from 'your native land'. Often they were confused about my actual identity. Long after the Mau-Mau troubles had died down, the memory still somehow lingered on in deepest suburbia. Always it was linked with atrocity stories, and a black face was enough to resurrect them.

'Are you a Mau-Mau lady?' I'd be asked.

And I had to reassure them, 'No dear, just a human being.'

They seemed relieved, and whispered, 'See, I told you she wasn't!'

'They've got spears. She ain't got no spear.'

'They got bows and arrows, as well.'

Some seven years after I left teaching, with my son and daughter growing up, I decided I'd like to have another look at schools. Just a look – I felt no burning desire to return to them. But I couldn't help but be curious. A new generation was entering the schools. Gone now were the children whose declared ambitions were to be spivs and Teddy boys. What was it all like now? I wondered.

So I decided to apply for admission to a diploma course.

It was now the sixties, the age of the frenetic immigrant, whom many older immigrants see as the grabbers, the plum-pickers, the protesters, the noisy people. The people who in some respects got off a boat into a virtual bed of roses and lost no time in trampling on it. Some of them became dupes of the failed and the power-seeking of my own generation.

Teaching, I soon found, had changed. The era of enlightenment had dawned. All the teachers I met on the course seemed eager to discuss, to probe and to ponder the mysteries of how children learned. And the emphasis now was on equality and discovery. Terms such as 'child-centred' and 'creativity' were flashed around like torches in the dark.

The one thing I hadn't imagined was the multiracial school. On my diploma course I learned about it at first hand from Bob, an overburdened, dedicated Headmaster who had been caught up in this phenomenon in a notorious slum area.

'My school is the worst one in the world,' he said. 'The children treat me and the staff the only way they know how to treat adults – like dirt – like the enemy – like the police. I've got nearly fifty per cent immigrant children. You name the country, we've got a representative.'

Living as I did in the suburbs, the creeping invasion of immigrant children in some areas and some schools just hadn't registered. I was fascinated by what he'd told me.

'Can I visit your school one day, Bob?' I asked.

'Come when you like. Just ring me up.'

'I'll take you up on that, one day,' I promised.

He was a fine man and passionately devoted to the underprivileged child. Although childless himself he respected the feelings of the young and the nature of their insecurity.

My husband and I became friends with Bob and his wife Marion. They lived only two stations away by Tube and so when Bob wasn't too harassed to concentrate, they came over to play bridge or just to talk.

I learned a lot about the school from Marion, who loyally stood in as a teacher every time there was a school crisis. There was constant staff turnover, many teachers being unable to cope with the new situation.

Some of the stories she told me were horrific.

'The children are looking for new anchorages,' she said, 'and so they go around in gangs. The parents are only really conscious of one thing – economic need. After all, that's why they came here and so they expect the kids to fend for themselves. It comes to the point where the parents just lose their grip and give up all responsibility for the children.'

She told me of a Jamaican child who had come to join her mother in England after staying behind for a while with relatives in her own country.

'This child expected what she'd been used to in Jamaica – her mother's time and attention, and security – all the things that her mother could no longer give her because she had to earn a living.'

And the child, naturally, having to fend for herself, had changed. Changed, in fact, according to Marion, to the point when the mother was asking the school to assist her in getting the child into a Home.

'I don't want her,' she'd said. 'She worst-up since she come here.'

The gang-age, Marion reckoned, began early. 'They won't

go near play-centres after seven or eight. They prefer the excitement of pilfering from the market shops.'

'Yesterday,' Bob said, 'the police came to ask my deputy to move his car and this in itself was enough to trigger off a whole series of confessions by quite half the children in the deputy's class about the crimes they'd committed the night before.

'These kids are completely disoriented. You could say that the state they're in reflects that impulsive act – that hasty decision that prompted their parents to send for them in the first place.

'It's not fair. They're right out of luck, these children. Why should they have so many disadvantages? Poor housing, ignorance, poverty, deprivations of all sorts.

'The only reading material some of them ever see is the *Greyhound Express*, the football coupons, and papers printed in Greek or Urdu. Then they come to school and we have to test their intelligence. They've got as much chance as a snowball in Hell.'

I had visited Bob's school and it was at the back of my mind, but at this time I was keeping in touch with young children in my own chosen way. I'd started a playgroup, which had succeeded beyond all my expectations although, at the outset, I'd had my doubts. Would white mothers take advantage of it, I wondered? As it turned out there was no problem at all. They were only too grateful for the service.

They paid me five shillings a week for three two-hour sessions and all in all I was kept very busy. So busy, in fact, that *I* had to get a mother's help.

'Advertise for one,' suggested my husband. 'Then you can pick and choose.'

Several women called but were unenthusiastic when they saw me.

''Ave to ask me 'usband, dear,' said one of them. 'Never worked with blacks before.'

'Rather serve me own,' said another, and so they came and went so fast that I began to despair.

Then one afternoon I opened the door to a tall, gaunt woman, with a hat slumped on her head like a nesting blackbird.

She didn't even wait for me to speak. 'Oh, it's one of you!' she said. 'I'd rather go to the National Assistance.'

'Jolly good luck to you,' I said, 'but it's a long walk from here. You'd better have a cup of tea before you go. It's made.' She glared at me and then stomped off. Her hostility, so irrational, and really so unnecessary, rather amused me. 'Sucks to you,' I muttered under my breath.

'Sucks to who, Mummy?' asked my son.

'Sucks to . . . well, no one. Never mind.'

Just then there was another knock on the door and when I opened up there was the same woman, blackbird hat and all.

'Now what?' I snapped.

'Think I will have that cup of tea,' she said, now smiling broadly. 'You see, I stubbed my right toe just after I left you – and I'm superstitious. So I thought better of it.'

'Don't force yourself to work for me,' I said. 'It's entirely up to you.'

She sat down, took my daughter on her lap and talked. I could see how lonely she was, but with her help in the flat every afternoon I was able to cope with the playgroup. It was a big thing to do at a time when our financial resources were so limited.

I made every learning aid I needed, as I'd given up the idea of being able to afford conventional play materials long before I started the group. And it was fun watching the children, their imaginations expanding, when they played with lids and buttons of all sizes, cotton-reels, twigs, wooden spoons, thimbles, plastic cups, cake-tins, beans and drinking straws. Conkers, macaroni and acorns were threaded instead of beads. The clothes pegs became dolls, people, creatures or ice creams. We used brightly painted stones for sorting and sharing, and made pictures from cereals, bird seed and grain mixed with paste. We sorted lolly sticks, dog biscuits and nuts of all kinds. Boxes, punnets, and broom handles, sawn into different lengths, were used for building, measuring and comparing. We were grateful for offerings of string, shoelaces, bark, straw and egg-boxes, all to be used in helping the children to think through handling, adjusting, measuring, comparing and constructing. A pair of old cushions, dressed in baby clothes, became Tubby and Blubby, who joined in our stories and played leading parts. They even advised us on how to convert an old Christmas tree into a Bird Breakfast tree. We dressed it with pieces of bread, balls of dough, bits of fruit and meat, and were all terribly excited when the birds came to eat – the blue tits with their dark coats glowing mildly in the sunshine, the pigeons with their greedy eyes and fussy feet, the thrushes in their speckled shirts and the sparrows pecking the bits with a kind of cunning eagerness.

At first the mothers found the lack of conventional play materials, as well as my efforts at getting the children to look and see, to feel, touch and talk with clarity and purpose, hard to accept, but as the children described what they saw with greater accuracy each day, and asked and answered their own questions, they ceased worrying. 'Is this worm squiggly, wormy and wriggly?' asked Victoria one morning. She paused and went off to look at something else. After a while she returned and said, 'Yes, it is squiggly, wormy and wriggly. It's a worm.'

The children enjoyed what I called the free-range material – material over which, at that egocentric age, their imaginations could range unrestricted by artificial boundaries of any kind. They handled, discussed, described and identified vegetables and fruit which I bought when the greengrocer called. They counted gloves and shoes, pillowcases and spoons in pairs, felt the texture of towels and blankets and old net curtains, so finding the differences between familiar things. They found visual differences between even more everyday things – salt and sugar, flour and oats, barley and peas, ice and snow, water and tea.

They looked at living things through our giant magnifying glass and learned to respect the right to live, and to sort out their own ideas about situations and objects.

'This spider has lots of legs, so it can go lots of places,' said Sarah.

'My tortoise has an egg shape. She'll go in an egg and hatch out again. So she'll be an egg-tortoise,' said Darla-Jane.

'I'm not putting this little snail in my book,' said Tom. 'He went out without kissing me goodbye.'

'I'm me – I'm not a baby and not a bird,' said Simon.

'This butterfly is the bride,' said Louise, who had just attended a wedding. 'Throw messy paper on her. But mind her dress. Now sweep it up. Sweep it up.'

'We're all animals in my house,' said Kim. 'We're all creatures, we're all people. We're not things. Things go bang when you throw them.'

'The sky is dirty. There's a big fog in a big sky,' said Simon. 'Call the birds. Call them home.'

All the rooms in my L-shaped flat were available to the children. From a music session in my bedroom where the piano was kept, they'd dash off into my living-room to feed the goldfish.

I became so engrossed with the children that I forgot the family luncheon cooking itself in the oven. At the smell of burning food I'd rush into the kitchen, the children all scampering after me. Kim, who didn't believe in wasting anything, often advised me to 'Save it up and give it to my daddy'.

Even at this early age, parents offered their preference in interests and ideas to their children, and were already willing them to like the same books. And I glimpsed how far back in time the seeds of conflict are sown. Sincerely wanting them to be like others, the mothers stamped on their children's individuality and talked at their children. Talking gave them control over their children and their situation. They said 'no' and 'naughty' easily and frequently and the children reacted in turn.

Tubby and Blubby were naughty by word and deed whenever they liked.

Tubby frequently complied with the request to 'say botty'. But on rare occasions he declined and said, 'I don't want to.' My daughter was always his mouthpiece.

Blubby on the other hand shouted, 'Pooh makes a stew!' at the most inconvenient moments. And then one day I made a stew with seven pairs of hands adding the ingredients. 'Blubby' learned how to really make a stew and refused his line.

Just before mothers came to collect their children, we played listening games. The quietness was described as weird, uncomfortable, uncanny. Parents expected noise. It assured them that their children were safe, well and happy.

We were going full speed ahead when an official from the Council called to check the accommodation. He referred to me as 'you people' but stopped when I pointed out I was only one person. He advised me to 'do the thing properly and move to the church hall'.

It was at that time that I decided to pass over the group to a mother who wanted to expand it. I was left with some equipment so I rang Bob and offered it to his school.

Entering his school playground was like being transported back to the West Indies. So many black faces everywhere. As I got beyond the gate the smell of the lavatories almost overpowered me, yet, right beside them, a group of black girls were skipping ritually. 'Eeney, meeny, miny, mo!'

Their version had a startling variation. Instead of, 'Catch a nigger by the toe,' they said:

> Put the baby on the po.
> When it's done
> Wipe its bum.
> Eeney meeny miny mo,
> You go out!

Further along, a group of Greek boys played cover cards for pennies. Where some children played for buttons, they staked pennies. When a boy lost his pennies he threw stones. It didn't seem to matter whom he hit.

Some black boys were enjoying their football. 'No whites!' they yelled when a fair-haired chap took a kick at the ball.

In my friendliest voice I asked one of them to take me to the Headmaster.

'No,' he said. 'You go up the stairs into his office.'

'But can't you take me to him?' I suggested.

'No, I can't. I have to give my brother his sweets.'

'Jolly good,' I said, 'you are a kind brother.'

'No, I'm not. My mother said to give him his sweets.'

Belligerence, it seemed, was all about me. I ran up the stairs and found Bob.

'Hello,' he said warmly, although obviously overwhelmed with work. 'I'm afraid I can't see you for a while. I've got a visitor. But Gareth's expecting you. He's in the far room on the right.'

I walked towards it and it was like walking into a kind of minor riot. It turned out to be the tuck shop and Gareth was under extreme pressure to provide quick service. Some yelled 'Sur' and the others 'Sah'.

I knew Gareth and liked him. Years ago I had attended a course with him. He had come into teaching through the emergency training provided after the war. Lively and interested, he was, like Bob, dedicated to the children but in his own mildly militaristic way.

The manner in which he spoke to them took some getting used to.

'Hold up your money,' he bellowed. 'Right up in the air. If you push, you'll have to buy from the rubbish tin.'

He banged a large tin beside him. It had a calming effect upon the children.

'What's in that tin?' I whispered.

'Nothing,' he whispered back. 'But some think it's rubbish and others ju-ju.'

'Why do you talk like that to them?' I asked.

'It's the only language they understand,' he said decisively. 'It's their public language I'm using. It's no use talking BBC to my little sweethearts here.'

'Oh, you're nutty, sur,' said a voice behind me. 'You bark bow-wow-wow all day.'

The boys scrambled out and a gang of overgrown, untidy girls replaced them.

'Back you bloody go,' Gareth yelled. He whipped a hand-kerchief out of his pocket and tied it around his face like a gangster.

'I'm allergic to the smell of sweat,' he said. The girls did smell sweaty.

'Not their fault,' he explained. 'The parents do the best they can, but they've got no bathrooms – most of them. I'm on their side, really, but I can't pretend. They've had to accept that as fact and I think they do. It's got nothing to do with race or colour – just the chance to make contact with water. I bought Lifebuoy soap for one of them, but she forgets to use it. She's without a word of English. I've tried to help her with that, too.'

'How about the West Indians?' I asked.

'Their failure is in their own heads,' he said sadly. 'They think themselves towards failure. For effort they substitute cheek and restlessness. I don't know how to take them or what to make of them. Some of them are bright but they don't believe it.'

'Do you go to their homes?' I asked.

'Yes, quite often. You see, I have to. I have to return the treasures some of them bring to school. Blue pictures, cigar-ettes, expensive rings, watches, money and so on.'

'Can't you get the parents to co-operate?'

'Well, it's difficult – very difficult.' Gareth spoke as if he'd abandoned hope. 'You see, letters frighten them and they tend to look upon what are mostly merely childish misdemeanours as utter disgrace. They say: "Why don't you beat the child?"

'Then, on the other hand, some of them have expectations which are quite inconsistent with the child's ability. Quite surprising – after they pass the poor kid from childminder to childminder before he finishes up here with us.

'I tell you, I feel deeply about these children but let's have no whitewash. Don't let us be hypocritical about their lot. They're born to be the bloody hewers of wood for the whole wide world. And they must tell the whole world NO!'

I went back with him to his classroom. I soon saw that his was a didactic system. He taught problem-solving as a skill, through rules. He had some gems on his blackboard.

To find the sum, we Add. Find the sum of eight and nine.
To find the area, we Multiply the length by the breadth.
Find the area of a room 6 yards long by 8 yards wide.

On the wall there were lists of spellings which had to be learned, and general information, like the days of the week and the months of the year, which had to be recited several times a day.

'When they know these things, they can paint and sew and do woodwork – not before,' Gareth said determinedly.

'It's the kind of teaching they'd get in their own countries,' I observed.

'I know,' he said. 'The others tell me that my classroom is a minor Dotheboys Hall, but a man must survive.'

It had to be said that the classroom was indeed peaceful and the children showed a sort of sullen interest in what they were doing.

'I'll leave you to it,' I said.

'No, I'll take you down,' he replied. Then, turning to the children, he bellowed, 'Clever Dicks, I'm going downstairs. If you move, put a counter on my desk and when I come back you'll tell me why.'

He said confidentially, 'All the parents expect the children to be docile, submissive, religious and clean. Life in these streets goads them into quite different directions.'

At the bottom of the stairs a pair of children stood waiting. One had a tear-stained face.

'Hello, Androulla,' Gareth greeted. 'What, crying again?'

'Sur, Lulu bite me,' said the little Greek girl. 'I said "Lulu, there's a kill-bird" and she bite me very hard.'

Lulu, the black girl who accompanied her, scowled.

'Sah, she tellin' a lie, sah.' She blurted it all out before Gareth could reproach or even greet her. 'She call me black-face, sah. She say: "Blackface, look at that kill-bird," and then her hand come by my teeth.'

'Well, to begin with, it's not a "kill-bird". It's a dead bird and yesterday you gave the same excuse. Tell me the things you ought to do with your teeth.'

'Chew my meals, sah.'

'And show them when you smile, Lulu,' I said.

'If you go on at that rate I shall either have to clout you or get your Mama-dear to clout you,' threatened Gareth.

'Mama-dear say if anyone clout me I have to clout them again,' Lulu explained. 'She say if Whiteface bite me I must bite them back.'

'You're the one who bites, Lulu,' he said, making a face at her. Androulla listened tearfully.

'Never mind, Androulla,' he said. 'Here, dry your tears and play with somebody nice.'

She snatched the square of tissue from his hands, made a rough ball of it and nearly poked it into her eyes.

'I won't play with Lulu no more,' she resolved. 'Only tomorrow I will play with her.'

Well, that, at least, was encouraging. She might talk prejudice but she had no intention of acting it out. They'd be friends again tomorrow. It's when such children acted as they spoke, I thought, that adults should worry.

'Goodbye, sah,' they said together.

'Poor Lulu!' Gareth sighed. 'She's unfortunate enough to be the blackest member of her family. She's also got what they refer to as "bad hair".'

'Yes, I know,' I laughed, 'kinkier than most.'

'Even her brothers and sisters call her Blackie,' said Gareth ruefully. 'And they're as black as spades themselves. Do you know? I've heard them call themselves "fair". Fair? They're all as fair as plain chocolate. The day I visited them Lulu's mother showed me this copy of *Ebony*. "Black is beautiful" it said in thick black type, but even before I'd left the house she was shouting: "Ella, come out of that sun before it makes you black." It was our English sun.'

I said goodbye to Gareth and went down to Bob. A small child lay on a bed in the corner of his room.

'He's sickening for something but he can't go home,' he explained. 'There's no one at home and so I'm stuck with him.'

'Isn't there a sick-room?'

'You must be joking. I don't even have a room for medicals. Everything happens here – here in my office. It's all terribly difficult.'

Tiredness came out of him in waves, but so also did an all-pervading warmth and humility. Here was a good man doing a well-nigh impossible job in the context of his own humility.

For the rest of that afternoon – long after I'd got home – I thought about these children, drifting like flotsam between old jettisoned values and values that were yet unattained. The blacks, more than other groups, had appeared to me as the most rootless ones in the system. They could have been my children sitting at the bottom of the class.

It should have been a most dispiriting experience. But somehow, in my heart, I didn't see it like that. Problems or not, it had challenge written all over it.

In fact, I thought, I'd like to work in a school with a multi-racial population.

One day, perhaps, I promised myself . . .

11

'Three cheers for group therapy'

The chance came much sooner than I expected and found me quite unprepared. Only a bare two weeks after I'd visited his school, Bob telephoned. He was desperate for help in his school. The influenza epidemic which had thousands of Londoners in its grip had presented him with his biggest staff problem yet.

'Several of the staff are away,' he croaked, 'and you know how it is. At the best of times supply teachers are hard to come by. One of them – a youngster – is in hospital.' He sighed expressively. 'The class she took made her ill. They've had seven teachers in as many weeks. So I'm putting all my cards on the table. Can you give us a hand?'

I remained silent for what must have seemed ages to him.

'Are you there?' His voice sounded cracked and tired.

'Yes, I'm here, Bob,' I replied, trying to adjust to what he said. It was like being asked quite abruptly to dive fully clothed into an icy pool. Was I ready for it almost at a moment's notice? Past experiences came rapidly to mind.

'I don't blame you if you say no,' Bob muttered, as if he could read my thoughts.

It was the despairing way in which he spoke that finally decided me. 'I'll come,' I said.

So, four days later, after several official telephone calls and a chest X-ray, I was able to start.

A bus strike made me late but I was still very welcome to the hard-pressed Headmaster.

'Thank goodness!' Bob greeted me. 'What a morning! I've spent the last hour chasing my tail. If you don't mind, make your own way upstairs. You'll find the children in that dark room at the end of that dark corridor.'

Put that way, it didn't sound promising. Nor was there much comfort in the little scene that followed . . .

Hurrying upstairs I turned a sharp corner and came upon an undersized West Indian boy, who said his name was Ezekiel. He groped about, collecting pieces of glass, whimpering as he did so.

'What's wrong?' I asked.

'I am sharrt-sighted and Roddy, Dinos and Sigmund push me and break me specs.'

Ripples of laughter came from the top of the stairs where three contrasting faces appeared.

'He's blind,' they cried merrily.

'Is that why you pushed him?' I asked in horror. 'Do you push blind people downstairs? No! Do you help them? Yes!'

They looked at me in astonishment as I asked and answered my own questions. 'Do you push people?' I demanded of them. There was a confused mixture of yeses and noes. 'Right, now! Come and help him, and don't you ever do that again. You might hurt him,' I said.

They seemed quite impressed by my anger.

After sorting out the problem of the broken spectacles, I reached my classroom. It was like a menagerie in which all the animals had gone stark, raving mad.

Class 2Y contained thirty-five youngsters, a few seven- but

most of them eight-year-olds. I'd always been convinced of my ability to control any group of children but when I stepped into that room my convictions about coping faltered.

The floor was littered with wax crayons, over which some boys skated and danced. A fattish boy stood on his desk bellowing, for no apparent reason, through a hailer which he'd made from a large map. Some children threw paper darts, while others simulated aeroplanes by running round with arms outspread and noise to match. A few children drummed on the desks. Others whacked books with rulers. A tall, slim boy ran around with his trousers down, to the delight of a small group of girls. In the midst of all the disorder a little girl lay quietly asleep, with her head on the desk. Some children just wandered around aimlessly, stopping now and then to strew books or pencils on the floor. The whole class welcomed me with a crescendo of catcalls and war cries.

I simply couldn't use size to subdue them. They were conditioned, like the rest of the world, to accept a hierarchy of size, strength and aggressiveness. I am only five feet two inches tall, anyway.

I decided to dare them. I walked straight across the room and sat at the table while obscenities, screams and shrieks banged away at my ears.

'Go on,' I said, waving at them. 'I bet you can't keep that up for an hour. It's half-past nine now. See if you can keep that yelling up until half-past ten. I couldn't do it. My poor epiglottis would be lacerated, but yours are made of iron, aren't they.' There was a slight uneasy simmering down. A sense of worry above the hubbub. What did I mean by that strange word? It was disturbing and even faintly frightening to some of them. Intent on spotting the leaders, I ignored the muted shouts and screams. In every class of Juniors there is always a Queen Bee – the one that all the boys love or would like to love. She is often fashion-and-clothes conscious, a bit narcissistic, and with a built-in ability to beguile.

I spotted her at last. They addressed her as Mandy or Mand. 'Mandy,' I called. 'Come here.

'You're smart and pretty,' I said. 'I like your dress. Is it new?'

'Yeh, I got it down the market, last Saturday,' she said, chewing away at her gum.

'Your mum lets you choose because you're sensible,' I said. This gambit paid off. She was now listening. 'Well, will you tell this lot of noisy babies that I'm here to help the Head. All the teachers have flu. No one else can come. I'm giving them five minutes – no, I'll make it seven minutes – to settle down. One minute for every teacher you've had, and then I'm going. I don't have to work for my money, you know.'

She gave me a sharp look and sidled off. A little Asian boy greeted me. 'Hello, Miss, I am glad you are coming. Now you will give me nice work to do.'

He smiled and shook hands. 'I'm Mandy's friend,' he explained, and off he went. Mandy skipped from group to group and child to child, trying to make an impression. Very soon she decided that this approach was hopelessly ineffective. Where she kept that mountain of rasping voice-power, I shall never know. She yelled, like a desperate fish-wife, 'Sit bleedin' down, the bloody lot of you! Put your bums where they belong, on them chairs, and do what she says. If you don't say nothink you can't go wrong. Do you want 'er to scarper? She doesn't 'ave to work for 'er money. She nicks it!'

'Three cheers for group therapy'

A mixed group surged towards me, smiling appreciatively.

'Do you nick, Miss?' a voice piped eagerly. 'Are you a good nicker?'

'Ever so,' I smiled. 'You ask my husband, I nick every penny he has!'

They felt let down.

'No, that ain't fair, that's not nickin', really,' a little fair-haired girl observed. 'Nickin' is nice. I nick in Woolworths. I nick sweets. I'm good.'

'Yes she *is*,' they chortled in chorus.

'Well, you can't nick when you're hungry,' I said, 'so let me mark the dinner register.'

'Not when you're hungry,' a Greek boy agreed. 'You must run. Sometimes they chase you. This lady, she is fat just like this' – he stretched his arms to their fullest extent – 'she can run. She chase me.'

'Well, more of that later,' I interposed, but they didn't budge. They wanted to talk, to confide, to share experiences.

'While I'm marking, I'd like some of you to read this like the grown-ups do, with your eyes.' I wrote on the blackboard:

> Children who scream in school let down their
>   parents.
> The Greeks let down their parents.
> The English do so too.
> The West Indians let down their parents.
> The Italians do so too.
> The Asians let down their parents.
> The Africans do so too.

'If you can't read it, Mandy will tell you what it says. She'll also tell you it mustn't happen again. Mandy, please make them a speech.'

'We all shame our mums and dads when we be'ave like little 'uns,' she shouted. 'We ain't eight months, we're eight years, so let's all do what she says. She's going to be our Miss.'

'It's up to you if I stay till your teacher comes back,' I said casually. 'I want to stay but I don't have to come and be ill-treated by you. I don't have to waste time. Your school is miles from where I live. I'm not having rowdyism. I don't mind you not knowing things, but I don't want you to come here drunk and disorderly.' They laughed. That was a concept they understood.

'Kids don't drink,' said Mandy.

'I do,' protested a West Indian boy. 'Me dad lets me have some rum. He puts it on my bread.'

They hung around me. 'Have your milk,' I said, nonchalantly. 'You can scramble for it if you like, or you can have it nicely, sitting at the table. Take your pick. The choice is yours. Good or bad.'

'Good,' they said.

Milk-time passed off uneventfully. Already they had begun to realise that all the choices would be theirs and that I was going to let them set their own standards.

I decided I would try to form them into loose friendship groups.

Groups, of course, existed already, but these were on a national basis. Roughly speaking, there were group leaders, too. Mandy and Peter, for instance, were the leaders of the English. Maurice and Sally led the West Indians. Shaim was the unofficial spokesman for the Asians, and Dinos for the Greeks.

All the children held strong opinions about the different races . . .

'I don't like Bubbles.' This was the derogatory name for Greeks and based on rhyming slang 'bubble and squeak'.

'I don't like Asians. They wear turbans and 'ave knives and they wash their bums in soap water!'

'How do you know?' I asked.

'Me mum says so. They make the toilets wet in her factory where she works.'

'I hate blacks – I don't mess with 'em.' This came from Mandy. 'Me dad says this is what you get when you mess with 'em.' She held two jelly babies in the palm of her hand – the black on the top of the pink. 'Black is the same as a bit of dirt and blacks pick their noses.'

'Turks smell of garlic. They have kebab in their pocket. They put the nail in people's leg.' Dinos meant the kebab meat skewer.

'Turks *don't* have kebabs in their pockets,' I said emphatically. 'They have money – pennies and shillings.'

'Turks *do*,' corrected Turka. 'I have kebab in my pocket. My mum give it me. Then I keep the nail. If anybody jump on me, I . . .' Skewer in hand, he showed me exactly what he'd do.

'I hate foreigners. They smell. They come to this country and make it smell.'

How was I to mix the national groups?

I decided to do it by a specially modified game of blind-man's-buff. First the children drew lots and those who had numbers one to seven were blindfolded and allowed to choose by touch other youngsters to make up their groups.

I stressed that once the choice was made it was final – 'You mustn't chop and change because it wouldn't be fair, and when you're seven or eight years old you *must* be fair.'

All the time I had to make sure that they understood everything clearly. If, at any moment, they seemed to be losing their way, they turned hostile and started to kick and swear.

The lucky 'choosers' turned out to be Louise, a West Indian, Mandy, Dinos, Henry, Androulla, Yacoub, a Pakistani, and Nipal, an Indian, whom they all called Nipple. He was so obsequious I felt like sloshing him.

Blindfolded, they made their choice.

'If I could see I wouldn't of chose you,' said Henry to Cathryn, a little English girl.

'Never mind. You couldn't and you did,' I said. 'Now I want you all to look very hard at each other and try to find something nice in everybody. If you see something nice, show your teeth.'

The most comic tableaux took place but eventually they settled down.

'And now,' I said, 'we must all be very busy. We're going to create a street market and each group must choose the kind of stall it wants to make . . .'

Soon even the most backward child became involved. The whole project excited them. Only Marion, the little girl who'd slept through the hubbub when I'd first entered the classroom, surveyed the whole scene listlessly. She had arrived only two days before from Jamaica and her sleep rhythm had not yet adjusted.

The children chose many different stalls. The flower stall was superb. The dictionary of wildflowers which had earlier been hurled across the room was now helping to meet an actual need. Some children seemed to have a special concern with fish and lavished much time and attention on this particular stall. At first they concentrated almost entirely on kippers and eels, until I reminded them of the fish shops and they were able to recite lists of fish to me.

Creating a dress shop delighted the girls and the boys who helped them make it. We talked about dress shops and dress designers.

'My mum used to be a machinist but now she's going to be blind,' said Kevin, a little Irishman.

'My dad's a designer. He makes clothes in the market. He says I will be a man-trap when I grow up,' said Naomi.

But even in their most involved moments of play a deep-seated desire for combat lay just below the surface of their minds. Proudly they told me that the class was no longer allowed to go into prayers because, in the past, they had caused a riot. I had to be constantly on the lookout for flash points, dousing them with humorous comment.

That afternoon we made picture records showing all the members of the groups. They worked with the utmost con-centration to paint replicas of themselves. The Greek children, I found, had a well-developed perception of form and fluidity of line. All used colour with gaiety and freedom. The black children made the most unrealistic pictures of themselves, showing features and characteristics they did not and could never possess.

By the afternoon playtime, however, regression had set in. The floor was littered with rubbish and the pictures had already been defaced. But no one owned up. We gathered up the rubbish and made a collage for the hall.

'Afterwards,' I said, 'I'll put pieces of paper beside each group picture and anyone may write their swear words on them. Be sure to use these pieces of paper only.' They seemed relieved to get that incident out of the way, and after a week the pieces of paper were still clean and unmarked.

As the days went by I found that playground duty had its own hazards. I had to be careful about the kind of games chosen for the children in this particular neighbourhood. I played 'Naughty Babies' with them, a game I played with my own children. It was the kind of game which by helping children to act out their unconventional behaviour in an atmosphere of humour and tolerance reduced the desire to be naughty. Within limits our 'babies' could do any of the things that were forbidden at home or at school and expect their chosen mum to react only with patience and understanding. It was difficult for some of them to control themselves and they would be halfway to 'See what you bloody done' before realising that the correct response should have been 'You're only a nipper'.

The babies were never reprimanded, or criticised, or corrected when we played our game. It was the only time some of them were cuddled, touched, fondled or hugged. Violence and aggravation came easily to the children and I tried to draw other responses from them by sometimes pretending that I didn't know what to say as mum. The onlookers, who enjoyed the game as much as the participants, helped me and called out, 'Miss, he lost his dinner money, you say, "I don't have no fuckinlope [f—ing envelope] to put it in."' 'Miss, you boil 'is balls for 'im.' Or 'I don't care 'bout your two-by-four teacher.' Without a doubt I had a good insight into some of the conversations that went on between the children and the people closest to them.

Sometimes the babies had to act rather than speak, and their actions were as violent as their language. Some could easily translate violent speech into violent action, and this made me try to find reasons for their behaviour, whatever it was. Many of the children lacked self-confidence and disliked themselves. As they grew older they saw the differences between themselves and other children, and transferred this hate to the environment, to school, to the teachers.

It was interesting to watch their body language. It was always harsh: two rigid fingers, fists at the ready, knees and feet eager to jolt and kick, and elbows waiting to prod. Any action which was considered soft produced sniggers or a sheepish 'I don't want to'.

But I always encouraged them and often they changed their minds and, much to my surprise, some of our babies did some 'soppy' things like kissing their mums because it was her birthday, or fetched money for her from 'up the Social Security', or told the rent man to 'piss off'.

Sometimes the naughty babies asked their mum to sing and as the song was invariably 'Baa Baa Black Sheep', everybody joined in. The singing and the game gave us a feeling of community and by spotlighting different kinds of behaviour helped the children, I hope, to understand why their parents acted the way they did when they were sad, or drunk, or tired, or afraid.

When we returned to class they were always in a mood to sit quietly for a while. I read poems to them and when I'd read one to them a few times I encouraged them to join in where and when they could. One day I recited a few lines from a poem I'd learned at school. It was called a 'gem'. The teacher sat near the door and we said our gem and then went out to play.

> Know you what it is to be a child?
> It is to believe in love,
> to believe in loveliness,
> to believe in belief;
> It is to turn pumpkins into coaches,
> and mice into horses.

At the word 'pumpkin', Dinos came to life. 'Miss, I see some pumpkin. You can buy it. I thief one and run to you with it.' Dinos relied entirely on his feet.

I realised that although I was saying that poem for myself, it had touched the children's lives.

'We got mice in our room,' said Henry. 'They done poo-poos in the rice.'

'We got mice as well,' said Mandy. ''Ave you got 'em, Miss?'

'I'll tell you what I have,' I said, 'but you can all try to guess first.'

''Ampsters, fleas, bugs, rats, goldfish, budgie,' they shouted one after the other.

'Wrong, all of you,' I said smugly. 'I've got a little nit, who is my son, and a little tit, who is my daughter.' They laughed heartily and were happy to go on talking.

'There's rats in my flat,' said Kevin. 'It's in the basement and the rats come in and eat my dad's toe. They smell stink. My cat is no good at all.'

'Tell me something nice,' I said. 'Do you believe in love like the poem says children do?'

'I believe in love,' said Androulla. 'You love God. I love God when I go to church in Camden Town. I kiss him.'

'When you love somebody you kiss them,' explained Mandy, as if she kissed God every day.

'And you give them chocolates,' said Nipal.

'And you take them up the pub,' said Kevin, 'and buy them drinks.'

'Do you talk nicely to them?' I asked.

'Sometimes,' they agreed. 'But sometimes you don't.'

'My mum and dad have words sometimes,' said Mandy. 'My mum always wins. I feel sorry for my dad sometimes.' Then, with adult resignation, she added, 'Ah well, can't be helped, I s'pose.'

I tried to draw out their ideas about other words in the poem. Horses they were convinced were up the betting shop. They didn't bother to follow up their thoughts on the subject, but when you said 'horse' the betting shop came riding on its back.

When I asked about coaches, I desperately hoped that someone would describe a family day at the seaside. But all they said was, 'We see 'em up the 'igh Street with grinny people in 'em.'

One-legged Hop, another of my children's favourites, was not only popular but useful. We played this game in the hall and the children had to hop behind 'mother' and then crawl on all fours every time she turned round. They were so exhausted by this that there was no strength left for disruptive behaviour in the classroom and getting them to wash their hands after-wards was no problem at all.

In a very short time some of the children had made consid-erable gains. They tried to find new work habits and to develop a 'reading attitude'. They spotted word-signs, notices and the names of their favourite shops. They made maps of their seedy surroundings and so found hidden interests in the decaying core.

I encouraged them to look more closely at their parents, to notice their radical and other characteristics and to learn their names. Few of them knew their parents' first names and were surprised by my interest in knowing them.

I read stories to them in serial form. I sang to them and they sang to me. Suspicion disappeared and tolerance took root.

Through art, drama and music they learned to appreciate and respect other cultures. For the first time they brought things to show and to share. Mandy brought her mum's gall-stones in a scent bottle. The staff began to wonder what had happened to the 'wild ones', as they were called. They thought I'd gone quite mad when I decided to eat with my class.

The secret was that the children had begun to realise that they were of more than passing interest to me. They no longer expected hostility in the adult voice. They began to be aware of my interest in, and my concern for their welfare. The ban on going into prayers was removed and, to the delight of the whole school, class 2Y told the story of 'The Pied Piper of Hamelin' and showed the pictures they had painted.

Parents came to see their large friezes which were hung in the hall. Class 2Y – miraculously, it seemed to the rest of the staff – had turned over a new leaf. All it proved to me was that children respond to love and decent treatment.

The children wrote individual diaries. Some were touching. Some frightening. Some amusing.

'I couldn't find my cat and it got shut in the fridge and it was froze and I cried.'

'Two girls put make-up on their face all day. Then wen' out all night and they fund the right man and they fund that love was horrible.'

'I saw two birds flying with their beaks together. They was in love.'

'Me dad beat me mum with a cup of tea. She pull his balls of neely. He said o-ow-ooo.'

'I wen to my ante and we eat and eat and we lafd and lafd and we didnt pick flowers becos they was stengin flowers. Me dad kiss me mum.'

'Me dad fell down and 'urt his back. Me mum sed "poor luv I sory for you." Me dad cried.'

'Me ante buyd a puppy. She put it on the chey. It shit there. Me ante sed now you go to the gutter. Me brother flink it from the window then dunstays. Me dad flink my brother out. See how you like it.'

Each child had a different concept of right and wrong. 'Do as you would like done to you,' I insisted, but few really understood this. I encouraged them to act plays with opposite themes – kindness and unkindness, happiness and sadness. But some certainly weren't kind to their pets and described glee-fully how they tormented them. Roland told me a harrowing story, 'My brother, you see, he catch this mouse in the trap. It weren't dead. He put it in with my tame mouse. They fighted. My mouse won. It ate the wild mouse and left the tail. I've got it in my pocket.' And he insisted on showing it to me.

Children who are socially handicapped and who lack close contact with adults – adults who will listen to them – need the opportunity to express grouses or confidences.

We had a book of grouses. It was kept locked up and the

ritual of obtaining the key and opening the cupboard gave the book an aura. The 'outsiders' had some odd impressions of the English.

'Engleesh pepul pick food from the grund and put it in they mous and eat it. They are dugs.'

'Englis pepl have strik sox. I hate them and they sox. Englis pepl eat snaks.'

'English people sleeping on the floor. Asian don't sleeping on the floor. English kill children with the nylon sox. It smell make them dead.' They nearly all mentioned smell.

Sometimes they wrote about their fears and dislikes . . .

'I don't like big tings and tick tings. The house is big and tick. I don't like the dor bell. It make me jump.'

'I don't like the big cowt wat people wear. In Cyprus we don't wer big cowt. You don't see your dad in the cowt.'

'I don't know my mum's nam. My dad calls her noting. I like my grandmother. Her name was Daysie Jones. I don't like my mum. She is crool.'

'I don't like going home. I think I wont no my house. I don't like the tolet. I don't like the chane to pull it. I hate the chane and the water.'

The English children had their say as well. The immigrants weren't alone in their efforts to pass on the stereotype.

'Foiners is nice but they should not come here till we invite them and we never will. Foiners don't work. They beg for money.'

'Me dad say Greks should be put on a ship and then a hol put in the ship. Greks are cheaters. They kill.'

'I hate people with forin ways. They talk horrible. Do you like them? I don't. This is our country. Forinas should go home, even Miss.'

'Black people live in trees. Me dad saw them isself. He was in the war. Black people rost people and eat them.'

'The Queen should send foreinrs home. She shud say, "You hop it or you get dun like we dun Jarmans!"'

Sometimes they brought me messages. 'Me mum says you're a foreign cow,' reported Sheila, whose mother was Afro-English. 'Really,' I replied. 'See if you can find a picture of a cow in any of the books on India and I'll know what I look like.'

Sheila had a large amount of water in her eyes and released tears at the drop of a hat. She returned sheepishly, holding a book. 'Here's a cow,' she said.

'Do I look like that?' I asked, amused.

'No,' she agreed. 'You don't, do you.'

'Well, that's a foreign cow, isn't it?' I smiled. 'It lives in India.'

'My mum said you eat cat food,' said Michael, 'and so I got this for you.'

'Thank you,' I said. 'I'll give it to my cat. But I'll show you when I'd eat it myself.'

I unfolded a UNICEF poster which I kept in my bag and which showed pictures of malnourished children. 'I'd eat it if I starved like these children. Wouldn't you?'

They gave up trying to be smart and worked very hard. The range of topics we developed was enormous. Bob was able to bring visitors to see us without first sending a courier to alert me. I was brought presents of all sorts. A handbag was even nicked for me from Woolworths.

'What shall we do with it?' I asked the class. 'Yacoub said he nicked it.'

'Pop it, Miss,' suggested Mandy.

'You can't pop a thing like this,' I protested. 'You wouldn't get twopence for it.'

'I thinking,' suggested Nipal. 'I thinking we must send it back.'

I agreed. 'Yes, we'll post it back. Yacoub, you and Shirley will come with me to the Post Office.'

It was a great outing for them. Yacoub even changed his shirt for the occasion.

At last Marion, our sleeping beauty, woke up and began to join in diffidently. I discovered that she was quite a gifted artist. She had an innate sense of pattern. 'But we'll have to get you more stamina,' I said.

'Oh Miss, they only put it in dog food,' Dinos informed me. 'I seen it on the telly.'

For days, Marion painted sheets of paper in vivid colours. Carefully she dried them and rolled them up. Louise helped her and they worked with a quiet intensity.

'What are you going to do with those?' I asked.

'To send to me grandmother. She want to paper her wall,' Marion confided. 'She only have newspaper.' Whether grandmother ever received her paper, no one ever knew.

Sometimes I was forced to ask quietly, 'Do you think Mummy can give you a bath tonight?' and after these requests the children always came clean and sweet-smelling the next morning.

At other times I had to suggest 'a change of underpants if you can'. The mothers co-operated as long as the children were happy. Many immigrant boys do not wear underpants and I had to be gentle in my efforts to encourage this. As Gareth had said, the smell from over-worn outdoor clothes turned into stench as some of them grew taller and sturdier. They were never blamed at the school for their inability to wash daily, yet it had to be impressed upon them that they must help their contact with other people by washing now and then.

The cold weather brought more illness in its wake and so my stay was prolonged. On some days so many of the staff were away that the school merely ticked over. If we were lucky we had a supply teacher or two. They varied in quality and concern to an extent which surprised me – once again a newcomer. Teaching seemed to have become a mere job of work. Since I'd been away from it something easily recognisable in the old career teacher appeared to have gone. I thought of it as a kind of feeling for child nature and a grasp of certainties.

I found, at this school, that I was never under the sort of 'colour' pressure from which I'd suffered in the past. However, although this was a multiracial school and I didn't stick out, not all members of the staff were as tolerant as Bob, or Gareth, of coloured pupils.

Some of the women teachers were repelled by the situation in which they found themselves. Their whole concept of teaching lay in dealing with a familiar situation – a white, working-class school. But now, a new situation had been wished upon them. They thought that the problems the children of different races brought to school certainly affected the way they saw themselves in the profession. They were no longer teachers but childminders, childcare officers and social workers.

Anna was the one who put this feeling across every day. She was a middle-aged spinster, a quirkish, positive woman who must have been beautiful when she was young. But now she was wrinkled and conveyed a sort of ground-in virginity. Her hands looked older than her middle years and had lost their softness.

I remember her lunchtime declamations in the staff-room. 'I feel great resentment,' she confessed once. 'I feel unutterable regret that the whole character of this school has changed. I can't wait to get out. I just can't cope. Look at this!'

And she passed an envelope to Mary, who sat nearest to her. Mary opened it cautiously and then went into simulated hysterics. Mary, a chirpy thirty-year-old, was like that. She fell easily into the role of actress. She would toss her fair hair as she laughed so that a lock of it fell appealingly over one eye.

But now everyone laughed as they peered into the envelope. When it came to my turn I saw that it contained a contraceptive – a rubber sheath.

'Sophie brought that to school,' Anna complained, 'and spent minutes blowing it up. Then that black devil, Dinah, told me with a grin, her mum has them at home and her dad puts them on his nice little head.'

'Sophie ought to see a doctor,' I insisted. 'It's dangerous putting those things into one's mouth.'

'Yes,' agreed Gareth, 'I'd take her down to the hospital. The clap isn't such a remote possibility around here.'

The conversation turned towards the changing neighbourhood scene . . .

'For years,' said Jill, another disgruntled teacher, 'I lived in my flat in complete amity, until this foreign dentist took over the flat above. Now I hate going home. It's endless parties, noise and visitors every weekend – tramp, tramp until I feel I'll go mad. Keeping the hallway clean and sweeping up his curry residue from round the dustbin, it seems, is my sole responsibility. You see, he is the wrong caste, so he can't clean up his own mess. I come to school so tired, I despair.'

'Have you complained?' I asked.

'Oh yes, and he said, "Why can't I do as I like inside my own flat?"'

Even Diana, small, dark-haired, and concerned for the children, began to remonstrate. 'We've got Greeks who run a home industry, although they know it's not allowed, on one side, and Indians who cook outside their back door, on the other. It's just jabber, jabber, jabber.'

'Surely', I suggested, 'something could be worked out so that people can understand each other and live together.'

'Who wants it?' cried Anna. 'I don't. This is our country. How would you like it if foreign people came along with smells, bells, mosques and clothes and swamped your tradition? Last Christmas we had a most awful time! The Indians banged all day. We couldn't even eat our Christmas dinner in peace, and here I am teaching their bratty children.'

'So what do you want?' I asked. 'Separate schools for these children? And as for *my* tradition, I haven't got one. Your ancestors saw to that. Anyway, you live in a friendly enough way with other people – Jews, French, Irish – why not with us?'

'They're white,' said Anna. 'That makes all the difference. Wouldn't *we* get discriminated against in other countries?'

'No, not at the moment. But you may later on if you go on like this. Never forget, children grow up – and children remember.'

'People will always discriminate,' insisted Anna. 'After all, you do it every time you go shopping, or help yourself to a biscuit or a chocolate. You can say you don't want what's black all over!'

'Yes,' I agreed, 'but it's not done just on colour. Shape, size, flavour all come into it.

'Would you let a room to *me*?' I asked her abruptly.

'At first I wouldn't have done – but now I would.'

'How about you, Mary?' I asked.

'No, love, I wouldn't,' said the chirpy one. 'I like you too much. Something might happen to make me think of you as uncivilised.'

'And you, Jill?'

'No, I wouldn't either. I'd be reluctant to share my loo.' She laughed. 'I've a thing about my loo.'

And not only you, I thought. I was now absolutely convinced that the entire British race had a thing about their loo. It must surely figure, objectively speaking, as one of the oddest of all national obsessions.

'Well,' I said, 'come to think of it, I don't think I'd choose to be a tenant with any one of you. You're too narrow-minded. And that might be catching.'

Their out-of-school reactions were less important than how they dealt with the children each day. In some ways their position was understandable. In an ever-shifting world, they wanted a status quo. Old patterns and old landmarks were fading around them. They were being asked to find new inter-pretations and it was all really beyond them. A school full of children from different countries was something they couldn't handle.

My reaction to such a school was, of course, utterly dif-ferent, because it represented school as I'd always known it, back home. There were five other races in our society – the Chinese, the Portuguese, the American Indians, the Hindus and the whites.

I had particularly enjoyed being at school with the Chinese, who set high standards of neatness and endeavour. There we all were – children of six races – in quite enormous classes of about sixty to seventy children, and yet I can't remember a single day that we ever quarrelled about race. If there was ever any jealousy, it was socio-economic in origin.

And so co-operation was possible. I knew it. I'd lived it.

Occasionally there would be a coloured face among our scanty and short-lived contingent of supply teachers. I couldn't get over the fact that an immigrant now seemed able to walk into teaching almost within hours of getting off the boat. It seemed a far cry from my pioneer days and desperate attempts to get started.

Well do I remember the day Mr Ali Rahaman came to help.

He was a rotund, bespectacled, grandmotherish man, about five foot six in height, and with black whiskers that gave animation and enigma to his face. He puffed his way upstairs, stopping to rest after every four or five steps. I overtook him, and because he tried to smile at me while he puffed, one of the buttons from his light black jacket went flying back the way he'd come.

'Hello,' I greeted him, 'you're losing your buttons.'

He didn't bother to retrieve the button but said, 'I am coming on three buses to this school. It is a very long way to come. My knees are very tired to climb the long stairs. The button is not valuable. I will pick it up when I am going down again.' He spoke with great precision.

'The stairs are better going down,' I comforted. 'Your class is next to mine. Just one more flight and you're there. Which part of the world are you from?'

'I'm Indian, but I live in Pakistan. I'm Muslim. I am going to see the children now? For me this is working as hard as a native.' He laughed.

'They'll be waiting for you,' I said. 'Hope you get on all right.'

'I will try. It is not too difficult to get on with little ones, only big ones are much difficult.' He wagged his head in a rather gentle manner, but soon I could hear him and his class at odds with each other.

'We want our milk – we want our milk,' they shouted over the mutter of Mr Rahaman. With some effort I managed to put him out of my mind and got on with my own work. I couldn't help him, really – I didn't know the class. It is important to know the names of children in a wild class.

After about half an hour I became conscious of an extreme silence next door. I rejoiced for Mr Rahaman. So he had subdued those fractious children. What was he doing with them? I wondered. He must be a genius to have 2Y2 so completely settled. I simply must see how he'd done it, or was doing it.

I knocked but got no answer. I opened the door. There was not a child to be seen. Mr Rahaman sat at his desk scribbling his thoughts on to an air letter.

'Where are the children?' I gasped. 'I thought you were managing nicely. Where are they?'

'They are spending some pennies and doing some creative jobs,' he replied calmly. 'They are wanting to do this.'

'You'll be spending some pennies if you don't get them

back,' I warned. 'If there's an accident you'll be liable. Those children are big enough to climb over the gate. Some will certainly be out buying sweets. Others will be rampaging in the playground. You had better go and get them back before any of the ground-floor staff start complaining about their antics.'

'I do not know where they are staying,' he replied without enthusiasm.

'Well, you'd better find out,' I told him. 'You are in charge of the class, aren't you?'

He was so casual. Finally he carefully folded up his air letter and walked out of the room, muttering a protest.

Mercifully the play-bell rang five minutes later.

Mr Rahaman puffed his way to the staff-room. After helping himself to a comfortable chair and a cup of tea with five lumps of sugar, he began giving us his opinion of his class in an unrelenting whine.

'These children, they are not respectful to me. I have one honours degree in history from the Ooniversity of Calcutta and yet they are not respectful to me.' His voice undulated from petulance to vehemence.

'They are asking me about my wives,' he lamented. 'They are telling me I must have only one wife or I must have seben. They are telling me the pork chops will give me strength for my wives, although I tell them I am Muslim. They are saying that seben dishes are better than one.'

Anna groaned in an effort to keep a straight face. Mr Rahaman gulped his tea noisily.

'They are telling me, "Do you eat with knives and forks? Do you have pant under your dhoti? Is your wife wearing pant under her sari?" And these boys they are eleben years old.'

201

'Maybe you weren't as inspiring in the classroom as you might have been,' probed Anna. 'You allow their innocent little minds to wander. It's your fault, whatever you got told, if you ask me. You let things get out of hand. Some of you lot are harmful to kids – whatever they're like.'

'That might be t'roo, what you are sying,' he countered, 'but these children they are also sabages – and uncontrollable sabages. In this countree there is eberything for their bellies, potatoes and tea and pork chop, and for their bodies there is shirts, collies and many such things but there is notting for their spirit. No one is caring about them.'

'How do you know that nobody cares? Have you discussed it with any of us?' fumed Mary. 'You accuse us of not caring about the children we teach!'

'Well, they are not knowing right from wrong,' said Mr Rahaman. 'A dog hangs his head when it is shaming itself. These children never hang the head. They are like flies and I am their cow for them to be irritating me.'

'Bull,' corrected Mary.

'Bull, cow, what does it matter,' he moaned. 'They are all the time irritating me. They will not be respectful to me. They have no understanding for me.'

'How can they when you stand in front of them yelling at them to shit down?' teased Gareth.

We exploded.

Mr Rahaman looked hurt and miserable.

'These children, they are not respectful to me,' he wailed. 'They are like their British grandfathers who were parasites in our countree. All the time they are dictating to me. They are not trying to learn. They are not wanting to do so.'

'Never mind,' I said. 'It's the same for all of us.'

He ignored me.

'This boy, Adolphus, he is telling me, "I want to paint." I give him paint and then he is spending his pennies in the paint in front of my face. He is saying bad language to me, and the others, they are laughing. I'm a teacher. I'm paid to be a teacher. I'm paid for my history degree – much money I am paid, and yet these children will not listen to me. I cannot tie all to chairs.'

'You make 'em listen, mate,' chivvied Mary. 'You said yourself you're well paid, so if you don't like it you can suit yourself. No one's holding you here.'

Mr Rahaman took off his glasses, stood up, and walked out, leaving a situation drained of all humour. The women were now on the warpath.

'The bloody bastard – the bloody Pakistani nit,' fumed Mary. 'Someone should wring his dirty neck.'

'The NUT should do something about bastards like that,' said Anna. 'Thank God for Peter Sellers – he takes liberties with them. Good luck to him.'

'I feel like spitting at him,' said another teacher. 'He's so bloody dogmatic. He shouldn't be allowed to touch kids' minds.'

'He just doesn't understand,' I said sadly. 'We're all on different wavelengths – all of us.'

I walked out and went to look for Mr Rahaman. I found him writing his letter again.

'The children are all right when you get to know them,' I consoled.

'I did not mean to be vexing anyone,' he explained. 'I am

holding the hand to all English people and children but they will not take the hand. I am only putting my points – not giving my needles.'

'You mustn't expect these children to be over-docile,' I explained. 'They live their own lives. Their parents are like shadows in their days and ghosts at night. They come and go.'

'To me these bery bad children are like the mules who will not drink the water when it is put under the nostrils,' he confided sadly. 'Indian children have minds like clean baskets in which we must put many flowers. In these children there is no humbleness, only poverty of heart and spirit.'

He left that afternoon, and next day Mr Dadusingh came. He was a very different cup of tea.

A young man, with a large hooked nose, he wore his arrogance like a suit made to measure, and he ruled the class with a rod of iron. I could hear him giving instructions like rapid pistol shot.

'Put your hands on your heads.' 'Copy this and not a sound from any part of you.' 'Stand on one foot and put your face to the corner.' 'Come here' – a command which drives fear into the heart of many an immigrant child. He felt free to treat the children as he wished.

He did not speak to any of us and did not pretend to understand the subtleties of teaching. He was paid to control the children and control them he did. He was a student of law, Bob said, and worked merely to supplement his funds.

But, late into the afternoon, the children felt they'd had enough. They rebelled in no uncertain manner. They dared him, they followed him around in groups, cocking snooks at him. They also stole his cigarettes and slyly smoked some of them. When he tried to smell their hands to prove his skill in detection, Adolphus, a Nigerian boy, scratched his face.

He flew into my classroom and in a despairing falsetto cried, 'That Adolphus, he is a black cat. He nearly tugged my face from my body.'

It was the first time he'd spoken to me. He continued making much of the scratch on his face whenever he could buttonhole a member of the staff. But the staff ignored him and were glad to see him go.

'He got what was coming to him,' said Anna bluntly. 'And now, after those two, I think I'll go and see the *Black and White Minstrel Show*.'

'Come home with me and see it for free,' I suggested.

'Don't be daft,' said Anna. 'You're no minstrel. But a show like that serves its purpose. I feel good after it. It makes me think of us and them in a special way.'

'How special?' I asked.

'Securely special – secure in my sense of tradition,' she said with pride. 'You can't beat a good laugh at others to set yourself right.'

She probably did need some sort of assurance, despite all her uncompromising talk. She'd told me, not long after my arrival at the school, 'I can trace my lineage back for four hundred years. I know who I am. Don't you worry. There's British, British, British blood in my veins.'

The time came for me to go. The teacher whose class I'd taken over had convalesced and would be back in a few days. I'd been at Bob's school for no fewer than sixteen weeks, much longer than I'd planned when I'd answered his cry for help.

The staff seemed genuinely sorry to see me leave and acknowledged the 'miraculous' reclamation of the wildest class in the school. They said my success was due to a 'common bond'. They meant a common colour bond.

'A common bond, yes,' I admitted, 'but I'd say that it was because the children and I shared the same quality of heart.'

'Anyway,' said Bob, 'you've been right for them. Would you come on permanently next term?'

'No,' I said firmly, 'I won't. My daughter has to have a tonsil operation so I want to be at home. And, really, I don't want to change my Local Authority.'

On the day I left Anna presented me with a book token for two guineas.

'It's from all of us,' she said. 'You've helped us all. It's been good, talking about things.'

'Good for you!' I said. 'And three cheers for group therapy. I despaired many a time. I thought you'd never see the shell in the sand.'

But that wasn't quite the end of it. During the Whitsun holidays that year my telephone rang and I heard a child on the line.

'Who is it?' I asked.

'It's me, Miss, Katina!' Instantly I remembered a little Greek girl in Class 2Y. 'Me dad look up your telephone last night. Can we come and see you?'

'Who's we?' I asked.

'Me and Mandy,' she replied.

'Yes, that's all right but don't come before three. I'll see you at the Tube station. I'll be going to fetch my boy from school. He hasn't had a whole week off, like you.'

'Three cheers for group therapy'

'Hello, Miss,' came Mandy's voice. 'We was in the park. Punch was cruel to the baby. I couldn't stand it. 'E sawed off its 'ead.'

'Have you been to the pictures?' I asked, thinking they were short of entertainment.

'I seen it twice this week,' she replied.

'Oh, come on then – as long as your mums know where you're going.'

At three o'clock I walked down to the Tube station, passing the prep school, in the very heart of suburbia, on the way. Already a crowd of suburban ladies were waiting to collect their offspring and I would join them, with Mandy and Katina, on the way back.

But when the train came, out from the compartment exploded not two but twenty-two children. I stood there amazed at this sudden reappearance of nearly half of Class 2Y. They carried bottles of Tizer, crisps, half-eaten oranges and Swiss rolls that were oozing out of their wrappings. It seemed to me that a few younger brothers and sisters, at the toddler stage, had been brought along as ballast. They all chattered and leapt about like performing monkeys.

'Cor! It's lovely round 'ere,' said Mandy, ever the leader as she began to marshal them. 'Evryfing is clean – even the grass.'

'Miss, this is my brother,' said Sophie. 'And Sugagonis is my cousin. Look him.'

'Hello, Miss,' peeped Henry.

'Where did you all come from?' I gasped.

'We was in the park,' explained Henry, 'then Tina said, "Let's go to Miss's house," and we asked the paper man which train to get on.'

'Where did you get the money?' I asked.

'We had it for chips,' Henry confessed. I shook my head at them but what could I say? Their very clear pleasure softened me.

Then I missed Dinos, unofficial spokesman for the Greeks.

'Where's Dinos?' I asked Katina. 'Wasn't he in the park with you?'

'No, Miss, he is in hospital. The men break his house and he and his mum had a new one. But every day he go back to this old house. He thinks his toys leave there. One day bricks cover him over and break his stummic.'

'Oh, poor Dinos!' I sympathised. 'He went in search of his memories.'

We all arrived outside the prep school and God alone knows what that snooty middle-class crowd thought of us all. Then my son appeared and the children leapt upon Paul and showered him with sweets and fruit, and the decorum of suburbia was sunk in a tumult of greeting.

'Ah, well,' I said, 'we'll all go to my house and sit in the garden. I'm afraid my daughter won't be there, though. She's gone to play with her friend.'

'Come on!' said Paul. 'We'll all have a super game!'

And that was what happened, with Tizer and crisps and soggy Swiss rolls to add to the party. As I looked out of the kitchen window at the children playing in the back garden, it was as if, for a moment, I saw beyond them and caught just the faintest, faraway glimpse of a multiracial society.

12

'Black, white, Paki, half-caste?'

I returned to teaching in 1963 as a part-timer and found it a weary and frustrating experience. As a full-time class teacher I had always been able to motivate both myself and the children. Each night I'd been able to reflect on the strengths and weaknesses of the day. But working part-time, it seemed impossible to make viable relationships anywhere.

In those days the part-time teacher was regarded by regular teachers as a general dogsbody or a kind of fringe benefit. And this attitude inevitably reacted on relationships with the children. I found that they looked upon me as little more than a shadow. Sometimes, when I was on playground duty, they flatly ignored me, and quite rightly so. I had little opportunity to learn their names and couldn't even address them properly. I was just the lady who took them when Miss needed free time, or was tired of them, or had something better to do.

The school was in an area of exceptional difficulty and many of the older children were at loggerheads with the law, their parents or authority in general. They destroyed equipment, broke windows and fought each other vigorously. In my early days at that school, a cluster of boys bombarded me with bits of ice, splitting my lip in the process.

The head was furious when he heard about it.

'Why did you do that?' he demanded.

'We didn't know she was a Miss, sir,' they said. 'We thought she was one of them spades from the paper-box factory. They swear at us,' one replied sadly.

So they apologised, their parents apologised and so did their friends. It all seemed to go on for a long, long time.

It was difficult not to notice that many of these children identified with members of their family who had already embarked on a life of crime.

I came across an example of this after I'd stopped a furious fight between two boys.

'What's all this about?' I asked. 'Now you write it all down and tell me.'

'I hit him,' the winner read out nonchalantly, ''cause he said he was going to burn down that nick what Dad's in. My dad's got a bad foot. He won't be able to run for it.'

The children's 'news' writing was, as ever, revealing . . .

Patrick wrote, 'My mum has another husband. When he comes I have to sit in the toilet till he wants to go in it.'

Sarah wrote, 'I hate my mum's boyfriend. His name is Desmond. When he comes to sleep I have to sleep in the bath. My mum makes a bed in it and the taps drip. I hate it when Desmond comes.'

In the playground the children reacted savagely at the slightest provocation. They passed on to me their parents' instructions – 'If that blackie touches you, kill him,' or, alternatively, 'My dad said do unto whites before they could do unto you.'

If words like tolerance, acceptance, self-control and argument had ever entered their vocabulary, the effects were invisible. They all overreacted. As for the teachers, when they could pin a label on their behaviour – perhaps 'deprivation', 'need-effect', 'disorientation' or 'culture conflict' – they felt free to disregard it.

'What can we do?' they said. 'We aren't trained to cope with this sort of thing.' They talked of children as if they were a race apart and of childhood as anything but a stage in human development.

One day, quite suddenly, I killed off my part-time teaching. I walked out and went home.

When eventually in 1965 I got back to full-time teaching I found no difficulty with new routines and trends. I found, however, that parental attitudes to school had changed. Teachers were no longer scarecrows in the field of education. Some parents bemoaned the passing of the eleven-plus.

If anything, the children had become even more colour-conscious. There was much talk of 'foreigners'. It was like dealing with an infection that had spread with time. A seven-year-old screamed daily when he knew that he was in my class. Nothing I said or did could pacify him.

His mother eyed me suspiciously. 'I've told him you're all right,' she said, 'but, you see, there's some around our flats. He's afraid of them. He thinks they're devils.'

Mercifully he was put in another class. He never looked at me but walked past with his head down. Perhaps he identified too closely with me; he had a conspicuous birthmark on his face.

During this period I extended my teaching in exciting new directions. I was interested in encouraging young children to write creatively, and I used handicraft of all kinds to build sensory thresholds and create concepts which children could put into words. Finding the words to describe with accuracy the textures and methods they used, in order to express their actions with clarity, was very difficult for them.

My own children were now nine and six years old, and it became an economic necessity that I should seek promotion. The children attended private schools in my area because they were accepted there, with tolerance and humanity. They never had to defend their colour or their hair, or bother about identity. Nor were the traditional names of affection, like Sambo, Topsy or Fuzzy, ever used to them.

So in 1968 I applied for a place on the promotion list and for a post as Deputy Head. Times had changed. Black teachers were no longer content just to be placed in the kind of schools that had a high staff turnover. I got my place on the promotion list and also a job as a Deputy Head. I knew it was only a matter of time now before I became a Headteacher, although I still felt reluctant to take on this ultimate responsibility for other people's work and actions.

But I hadn't bargained for the impact that my new school was to have on me. It was an utterly inspirational experience. And it changed my attitude to responsibility.

Since I'd helped Bob, the multiracial school had always been in mind and now I was Deputy Head of just such a school. From the start it seemed different from any other school in which I'd worked. I felt this on my first visit. I was struck with the ease of interaction between staff and children and between child and child. There was no pretence here – no shows were being put on. There was no playing to the gallery.

It was an infants school of about three hundred children from many different countries, set in a working-class area with many of the related social problems and emotional pressures.

Poor housing, overcrowding, fecklessness, had all left their mark. Most of the children were fiercely independent and needed to feel independent at school. So there was no use ordering them about – inhibiting them or shackling them with too many restrictions. The rules had to be few and definite, and, what was even more important, the children had to accept them emotionally. If they didn't, they isolated themselves from all that went on about them.

Beryl with her class at Tufnell Park School,
London, 1968

But the fact was that they loved school. It was a place where they could find solace, comfort, refuge and friendships of all kinds.

It was a school in which teachers were valued. Their well-being was of keen concern to the head. 'If the staff are happy the children can only benefit,' she said.

She was a remarkable woman. Jolly, forthright and in her forties. She had four children of her own. Above all, she radiated optimism and a kind of joy, and managed to communicate it to children, parents and the rest of the staff alike.

She didn't expect teachers to 'know their place' so that they stood on one side of a line while she stood on the other clutching a presumed omnipotence to her breast. Rather, the emphasis was on sharing a common philosophy of education. The fact that I'd brought up my own family counted with her. No longer did I have the feeling that I was the eternal apprentice.

Each morning we met in her office, chatting about the children, their foibles and our failings, their strengths and our weaknesses. We discussed our assumptions about them, and our own ability to cope. Through trying to understand the children we came to understand ourselves. We shared in democratic decisions. This school was run for everyone. It wasn't the Headteacher's kingdom – a place where she could enjoy a daily ego-trip.

The staff understood especially the children's need for love and warmth. Some arrived at school almost smacked to shreds. Some arrived still bewildered with recent experience – 'Me dad cut hisself off me mum's wedding picture. I don't know why he done it.'

Others came deaf to ordinary speech. Suddenly pitched into a new world, they still listened for the familiar speech patterns and did not always make sense of English words and sounds. There were problems everywhere but for some children problem-solving was always a group activity. Every member of the 'family' was expected to make some sort of contribution to solving a particular problem. I remember a little group of Asian children trying to clarify a situation involving lost dinner money. There were seven of them and each contributed one word of the sentence: 'His-pocket-got-one-hole-money-lost.' It was all they could manage but they managed it between them.

Other children came conditioned never to give answers unless they were absolutely certain they were right answers. So, before we could teach them any skills, we had to make them feel that talking for its own sake was important. We helped them feel that they were a rightful part of the jigsaw that was school. The staff never assumed that children brought nothing of value to the school. The concepts and skills – all necessary to achieve in their new society – would come later. In the meantime we provided them with the opportunities to hasten the process. We took them out. We talked to them. We played with them. We read to them. And we accepted the parent-role whenever it was thrust upon us.

Because most of the parents were out at work the children relied on the school for emotional support. Parents left for work even before the children set off for school and so these infants wandered the streets, sharing swear words as if they were sweets, and invariably arriving late for class.

The head never pretended that problems didn't exist but neither did she parade didactic solutions. She urged us only to look upon the children with a full consciousness of our own prejudices and limitations.

Each racial group had experienced a different pattern of 'mothering'. Many children were used to seeing their mothers being beaten by their fathers, or by their boyfriends.

A black Community Relations worker called one day and we discussed the attitude of black parents.

'They think they've failed even before they've set a life-course,' he said. 'They hate this society and when their children bring it home they hate the children. Too many have to watch their hopes for their children fall away and die.'

'I wish they'd ask us what books to buy,' I said. 'So many buy the kind of encyclopedia that nobody could read.'

'You know, man,' he said, 'we think the harder the book the more cleverness it gives. Some children born to that kind of persecution.'

He'd just left when commotion erupted in the corridor. A pregnant mother had begun labour pains. We made her comfortable and sent for her husband. After a while a fussy, complaining little man appeared.

'This is a welfare state,' he said. 'The doctors and nurses are able to look after her.'

He was most annoyed at missing his lectures – he seemed to be a student of some sort – and treated the whole business with the utmost contempt. His son was in my class and the boy tended to bully the other children. Now I could see why as the father literally dragged him off home, snapping orders at him. It was enough to set the other children off on a discussion about their parents. On this occasion they talked of the different ways in which their parents punished them.

'My dad hits me with a belt,' said Derek, 'then he soaks me with water.'

'My mum ties me up to her chair with her kerchief,' said Ahmed. 'Like a cowboy she tie me up.'

'My mum make me kneel down and then I 'ave to 'ave a

book in this 'and and in this 'and,' said Kevin. 'It ain't 'alf 'eavy.'

'I get bread and water,' said Akin, whose dad had been a prison warder in his own country.

'My mum give me senna-pods, then I have to stay home,' said Dorian.

I steered the conversation to rewards.

'Now tell me about the nice things your mums give you,' I suggested. 'Do your mums kiss you?'

They all tried to speak at once.

'No, I too big.'

'No, I'm a boy. You mustn't kiss boys. She kiss my dad, though.'

'I kiss my mum – she's nice.'

'I have a boy,' I said, 'and I kiss him. And my daughter kisses her dad. You see, we're a family.'

The Head used to visit the children's homes and was on friendly terms with most of the parents. I don't think the question of race ever arose in her dealings with any of them.

For my part, I tended to lose my patience with some of the West Indian children, particularly those who came late to school. I insisted that equality of expectations at school, or in the world outside, meant taking equal responsibility.

I pointed out to black parents that asking me to make allowances for them cast them in the role of problem people, and if I ever saw visitors patronising black children, I could barely keep myself from objecting. I felt that in spite of our difficulties in living and coping, we blacks *ought* to encourage our children to make demands upon themselves, to assess what they were actually getting from school and to use the system for our advancement in the same way as other immigrants do.

My own view is that some white teachers quite innocently help blacks to perpetuate their stereotype by being too willing to 'understand' problems, to make allowances, to turn on an ever-ready sympathy tap.

I tell the parents of the subtle implications woven into such phrases as, 'He's a lively child,' or, 'He's helpful,' or, 'He's developing,' or, 'He's jogging along.'

From my experience, a 'lively child' is one who doesn't spend a moment at any given task, a 'helpful child' does all the non-academic classroom chores, a 'developing child' or one who's 'jogging along' spends all day chasing his tail.

Parents of all races just wouldn't attend 'medicals', although we worked hard to convince them that the children were totally unable to answer questions about their babyhood. All the children could do, therefore, before these 'medicals', was to give the Head as much of this information as they had, and then she would stand in as parent. The children accepted her in this role. I think some even preferred her.

The staff at this school, without exception, really loved the children. It was here for the first time that I saw teachers actually nursing children and making cups of tea for those suffering from overexposure to the cold of winter. The staff-room was the place where children could find help if they needed it. They approached it joyfully. There was none of the traditional 'chasing off', at which so many teachers excel.

We knew full well that for quite a time after coming to school the newcomers would continue to think in their own language and draw upon their own group values. We tried, therefore, to engage the children in such a way that they felt new needs and sought new answers.

But we didn't always succeed. There were mental and emotional blockages, some embedded deep, others arising from incidents which happened before they came to this country. Samlal was a case in point. The mere thought of an outing to the zoo made Samlal sweat and cry. The zoo, to Samlal, meant the jungle from which a jackal had come, torn a hole through the fragile hut in which his grandmother lived, and bitten her in the neck as she'd lain asleep. He'd seen her mangled body and now a fear of wild animals seized him even if he only saw them in books. When his father explained his fears, we readily understood.

It was necessary also to understand how each group reacted to what we would normally take for granted. For instance, witches were not to be spoken of lightly at story time. As far as the Africans were concerned, witches were a real experience to them. They were creatures to be feared. Nor would Greek girls take on the role of witches if we staged a little play. Similarly, the West Indians would reject the roles of slaves or servants. Sometimes we found we had to alter nursery rhymes and edit familiar stories so as not to offend the children or their parents.

Some of the children disliked British food but for most of them school dinner would still be the main meal of the day. So we tried to encourage rather than compel them to eat. Some came to school bearing the weight of their parents' worries. If there was unemployment or illness or upset of any kind it showed in class or playtime behaviour.

Parents were frequently being evicted at a time when the Social Services were overwhelmed. The teachers tried to find practical solutions. Often, to cope with an immediate crisis, they would take children home with them, sometimes for several days at a time.

Constant pressure from officialdom had scared many parents off letters and printed matter in general – except, of course, the Pools.

'Every letter I get', one father said to me, 'is to tell me something bad. I hate letters.'

We had to wean them away from this fear and so we sent them cheery notes about their children, telling them good things and creating talking-points between themselves and their children.

My own mixed class of sevens and a few five-year-olds were devils – loyal, lovable, totally enchanting devils. They came in all shades from blonde to boot-black.

I spent a lot of time trying to make the first hour at school their happiest time of day. Once, in a fit of despair, I played them the music from *Peter and the Wolf* and told them some of the story in a dramatic – perhaps even terrifying – way. Those who didn't understand the words at least understood my gestures. And those who understood neither words nor gestures understood the ghastly sounds I made. Suddenly I stopped and said, 'That's Part One – Part Two tomorrow if you come early.' They did. And, afterwards, they painted pictures of the story. They painted fantastic mind pictures of Peter, the Wolf and Grandfather. The pictures they painted were truly sensational. Three of them won places in the *Daily Mirror* Art Competition that year.

The teachers took 'school' home to their families. My family became really involved in it. They loved to listen while I recounted my class activities, and would often visit the school to see it all for themselves.

Since my class contained so many nationalities I had constantly to remind myself that I didn't share the whole culture of all the children. I could not regard them as deprived. To do that was to overlook all the learning and stimulation they'd received before coming to a British school. Similarly, I had to accept that the situation in which they now found themselves could often be one that provoked anger and frustration in them and their parents.

They never had difficulty in finding words best fitted to express their emotions and so I set aside a seat we called the 'swear chair'. I urged them to use it rather than slouching, swearing away in corners. But they became self-conscious about it. They still preferred a corner, particularly for rude rhymes. One which was quite a favourite for a time went:

> As I walked down the country lane
> I had a niff of kippers.
> I asked a lady what it was,
> She said, 'Cor, it's me knickers.'

We never stopped them reciting their rhymes because we regarded them as an illustration of their own humour, their attempt to secure an audience and encourage its participation, and to get my full attention. It was their language practice and for them an achievement in verbal expression. Nice English poems had no connection with their lives.

When I joined them at playtime they insisted on teaching me skipping rhymes. While they skipped they'd listen to see whether I'd got them correctly.

Rosy apple, lemon tart,
Tell me the name of my sweetheart.

For this one they'd stop the rope at different letters and guess a boy's name which began with the chosen letter. And then there'd be a sort of supplementary question – 'Black, white, Paki, half-caste?' If anyone got one of the not-so-favoured races there would be a lot of general tittering.

I found that the Greeks, Italians, West Indians and indeed some other groups had well-defined roles for males and females. For instance, they accepted the engaging male rascal – adventurous, rough and bold. In strict contrast they expected girls to be modest, resigned and submissive. This obviously presented problems for the boys. At school they were under female dominance, and obedience, order and quiet were, to some degree, required from all the children, regardless of sex. The boys from the Mediterranean families were lions at home. At school they saw themselves as eunuchs in the power of a woman teacher.

'Do you cry, Miss Gilroy?' asked Gino. 'My mum does when my dad does this!' He pounded the air with his fists.

The Head often reminded us, at times of stress, that having a hard time was a two-way experience and that children who had to change home-behaviour for school-behaviour were perhaps having the hardest time of all.

Without question, the frustration felt by those who had no English whatsoever must have been colossal. Many were tearful and confused and clung to their coats and personal possessions. These at least gave them some sort of identity and sense of security. Some, of course, were wearing shoes all day for the first time in their lives.

We had a teacher who specialised in teaching English to those children who knew nothing but their native tongues. They were taught through a combination of activities – cookery, arts and crafts, dance, drama and music. Parental participation was encouraged and as much as possible was done to provide links with the home. Parents were invited to school activities such as puppet shows, and these provided talking-points for parents and children. There were also school outings to the pantomime and to the seaside. The children were taken around the local shops and shown books about London and maps of the Underground. Everything possible was done to help them to absorb a different way of life. The amount of progress made by the children varied according to the amount of stress in the family, and particularly as regards the support the mother got from the father.

New insights were constantly being given to us by the children and their parents. One mother confided her reason for advising the youngest of her six sons not to put school dinner bananas and custard 'near his mouth'. It seemed she had something special marked out for this one and therefore thought he needed a more 'virile' diet.

'He is me "wash-belly", Miss Gilroy,' she explained. 'The last one what wash out all the pregnant from me. When 'im grow to a man I want 'im to be a fine strong he-man.'

A father said, 'You see, teacher, the children don't value school. Back in Trinidad when I was a boy I go barefoot to school. The road so hot I walk barefoot on the grass. Sometime I hungry – my mother don't have a penny to buy food. I work as yard-boy. For my wages the lady learn me to read, give me clothes and food. The children got it fat nowadays.'

Black parents, in particular, seemed suspicious of the school system since it didn't correspond to their own school experience. Where were the homework, the punishment, the lashings?

'I ask 'im to say his ABC,' said one mother. "Im never hear such a word. Ask him ten and ten is how much, 'im count 'im fingers then 'im count 'im toes he said they was ten each.'

The parents expected the children to chant the alphabet as they did in their homeland where the ABC was the first step to learning to read. They also placed great importance on counting out loud.

'What worry me', she added, 'is that he's not afraid of the teacher nor no God-person. We beat him, him worse up. All I do is cry and pray over him.'

At the meetings with parents we tried to explain that going to school wasn't, and needn't be, like drinking castor oil. But still some wanted us to be sterner, to frighten the children, to chastise them.

'Licks put goodness in the soul,' they maintained. Some of the West Indian mothers ganged up in a tight clique born of shared opinions. They felt they were doing a good job if they fed their children, physicked them, punished them and warned them about whites. And should they run into problems their attitude was fatalistic. 'He born that way, man, he born that way.' This would be said with much head-shaking and sorrowful, downcast eyes.

Mothers of all races seemed lonely. They often confessed, 'Today I haven't said a word to a soul.'

Most of their men did night work or shift work. Some had two jobs and their only normal contact with the family was at weekends. The few women who hadn't got jobs of their own were bored and frustrated. Sometimes loneliness, and fear of the single, cluttered room, drove them out of doors into a habit of loitering around the school.

This sort of frustration sometimes boiled up into hostile argument. On one occasion, I watched two young mothers fighting like angry cats. Afterwards they helped to put up a sign saying 'Do not argue here' in Greek and in Turkish. They read it, and tittered, and then argued about the handwriting.

Out of this situation arose one of the most amusing incidents I ever witnessed in my teaching career. One day, a young Greek mother, whose hair normally swung heavy, black and sleek, turned up at school in a red mini-skirt with her hair as blonde as a cornfield. She loved herself in this new, surprising gear and she pranced along the corridor like a crowned peahen.

A cluster of waiting mothers stared at her and it all seemed too much for one of them – an old enemy. Up boiled the argument, back and forth flew the incomprehensible words, and, in no time, the spitting and the hair-pulling were well under way, and alas! the blonde wig was snatched off. The opponent held it aloft, then swung it around and around in the style of a hammer-thrower.

Extraordinarily, everything then dissolved into laughter with every mother trying on the wig in turn – until at last it was returned to the original troublemaker. The second time round it proved too much for her. She threw the wig down and stamped on it and so the fight began once more. In the end I had to break it up with the help of the children. It was obviously a shameful thing to fight in school so the mothers drifted off in disgrace. Eventually a group of them came back, and now very much in the manner of shamefaced children they asked me not to tell the Head about the fight.

So we sat down – all of us – and had cups of tea.

That was the day also when we suffered one of our relapses into more traditional racial controversy.

Back with the class, the children told me dramatically, 'Miss, Lena's come!'

There was a touch of drama here since Lena's father had adamantly refused to send her to school if she was going to be taught by me, a black teacher. I knew that an argument about this had been going on for weeks between this man and the Divisional Office. The staff hadn't told me of it but the children did.

Now young David laid it on the line again, 'Lena's daddy don't like black people. He told her she could hate them, too.'

While I looked at Lena, sitting there, tense and ill at ease, a hearty discussion on colour brewed up in no time at all. There seemed quite a lot of support for Lena's dad. So strong, perhaps, that soon some of the brown children felt constrained to say they didn't like the blackish ones. This got the black ones concerned and before long we'd reached the point where even the blacks were saying they didn't like black. Or rather, the lighter shade of black began looking around and condemning the darker gradation.

'I like Humans,' I said. 'Have we got any Humans here?'

Nobody answered.

'You're all Humans,' I said. 'Human beings.'

'Cor!' said Gogo. 'I'm Greek boy – I think!'

'I know!' said Trevor, looking down at little Gogo significantly. Trevor was a hefty West Indian with a well-deserved reputation for his powerful thumping. Little Gogo was suitably wary and respectful.

Poor Lena! None of this helped her. Straggly-haired and tight-lipped, she clutched her dinner money and whimpered about her mummy. She could find no calm or comfort anywhere. She wriggled and jiggled and it wasn't long before David warned her, "Ere, don't piss 'ere!' and Sharon, from Jamaica, whose mother was a nurse, aired her superior knowledge by announcing, 'Miss, she's done her urinade – but she can't help it.'

'She's wet herself,' I said firmly.

'Yes,' said quiet and logical John, 'with pee.'

The lavatories were a long way down. Wetting was often unavoidable. No one bothered about it. We wiped it up and changed the children. They felt bad at such times and worried that their parents might find out.

Every day I watched little Lena struggling, as it were, in some dark tunnel of the mind.

One morning she seemed a little lighter in mind.

'I wanna paint,' she said. 'I want oo.'

Later she struggled with books. There was a quiet and brave determination about her that impressed me. But I still got the occasional whiff of gunsmoke from the home front.

'I 'ad a caterpillar in my salad,' she informed me after one dinner-time. 'My dad says you eat 'em!'

I did my best to start her reading but, then, teaching the children to read was a prime concern. I realised I could take them through the reading scheme – rather like putting dogs through hoops – but this wasn't anywhere near good enough. Too often the children brought to school a flat indifference to books. Some had never even learned to turn the pages, or hold them properly.

So we started a book club for them. Children's books. Paperbacks. And we were delighted by the response this won from the parents. Mothers and fathers of all races would chatter excitedly as they examined the books. They would stroke them, even smell them, and invariably they would purchase one or two. I think they even read them – I knew the simple pictures amused them. 'My mum read that book what I buyed,' one little girl told me.

Beryl reading to her class as Deputy Head of Montem School in Finsbury Park, London, 1968

A West Indian mother explained, 'You see, the body gets old but the heart never gets old. It gets sometimish, but never old. My heart always tells me to buy books for the children.'

And then she added, giggling like a schoolgirl, 'But me, I

like romance books, man – Barbara Cartland. When I'm on night duty, I read them. I work with old people.'

Lena continued to worry about her reading but seemed a little less tense as the days went by – that is until one morning a group of children came running up to me with another of their dramatic announcements. 'Lena's mum coming up, Miss,' said the spokesman. 'I sawed her.'

Immediately the child tensed up again and started to stutter a question. But before she could get it out, her mum walked in. She was neat and trim, with her hair carefully put in curlers. Her carpet slippers were brand new. She looked like Lena in thirty years' time.

'Can I help you?' I asked.

'Yeh,' she replied. 'I was up the launderette and I found I left my key indoors. She has hers. I want it.'

'M-m-mum, what you want?' said Lena, as if a key couldn't possibly be all of it.

'Your mum told you,' I said.

She wriggled out of the key around her neck and handed it over, dangling from its long calico strip.

'She's a nice girl,' I said to her mum. 'It's a pity she's missed so much school.'

'It's me 'usband, see,' she said. ''E's got 'is ways and 'is idears and 'oo am I to change 'em. 'E's 'ad them same idears since 'e was a little feller, so 'is mum says. I can't change 'em now, can I?'

Lena tittered nervously. She'd obviously heard it all before.

'Me dad don't like blackies,' she explained, in a spurt of outspokenness. 'That's why I couldn't come to school. 'E didn't want you to teach me nothink. A man kept coming round'

– this was apparently the School Attendance Officer – 'Me dad 'ad words with 'im.'

I shrugged and Lena's mum looked sheepish before shuffling away in her carpet slippers.

And that was how my class launched into a discussion in depth on Mr Enoch Powell.

'Me dad likes Mr Plowle,' explained Lena, now in full spate. 'Mr Plowle lives up Parliament.'

'I know Mr Plowle,' said Angie, a gangly West Indian girl with her hair in neat clumps. 'He don't live up no Parliament. He lives round by our pub.'

''E don't live round your pub,' interrupted hefty Trevor in his down-in-the-boots voice. ''E goes to my church and 'e plays 'is banjo, and dance with my mum.' He did a little jig to show us how.

''E's my friend,' said little Gogo, the Greek, amiability shining even out of his sleek black hair. ''E say, "Gogo, goin' your school?" I say, "Yes, I goin' my school." 'E say, "Good boy, Gogo! Afternoon, come in my house, play with me."'

'Tell liar,' said Andreas. 'Mr Plowle and my dad is friend. I like 'im – and my mum and my baby like 'im.'

'I don't like 'im,' said Sheena from Grenada. ''E's got a bad-talking mouth. Me dad told me 'bout 'm. 'E said black people put cackie in boxes.'

'Black people no done that. Mr Plowle he done it,' said Gogo, probably fearing a thump from Trevor. 'I sawed him. One day my mum buyed some cake, in one box. Mr Plowle, he take it. He put some dog shit inside.' He illustrated with his hands.

It seemed high time to switch the conversation. We always worried at that school when immigrants became political fodder. When some of the parents felt that people in high places backed up their particular beliefs, relationships deteriorated. One or two would ask pointedly to see the Headmistress. If she was away they made it quite clear that the Deputy Headmistress would not do. They'd walk out muttering, 'I don't 'ave to tell you what I want,' or, alternatively, 'Why should I 'ave to tell you? It's private.'

'Come on, now,' I said, changing the subject. 'Who's going to tell me a nice nursery rhyme?'

'Me! Me! Me!' they all shouted.

I chose Sheena. She smiled, swung from side to side, and said, sniggering from behind her fist:

> Fat Mistah Kelly got a pimple on his belly,
> And his wife cut it off and it tasted like a jelly.
> Ladies and gentlemen it's ever so nice,
> Pull down your trousers and slide on the ice.

'Well done!' I said, masking a feeling of acute surprise. 'Now, back to work.'

At the end of that day Lena came up to me, all smiles, and put her arms around my neck. 'Tomorrow,' she said, 'I'll bring you some chocolate.'

She did. She brought something else as well. It was a magazine.

''Ere you are, Miss,' she said. 'My big brother gived it to me. 'E don't want it no more.'

'Well, put it with the others in the pile,' I said, and I didn't give it another thought until, later, I saw a group of boys hunched over it, rocking with laughter.

'Dinos, why are you painting a picture-man's cocky?' asked fellow-countryman Costas. 'And he's nekkid.'

I looked. Yes, why indeed? Furthermore, it was being painted, most carefully, in yellow and green stripes. The magazine that Lena had brought was a nudist magazine.

'You must take that home when you've finished,' I said. 'You must show your dad your work, mustn't you?'

This set the boys off in another bout of helpless laughter but the girls stood aside quietly, taking only shy looks. It was as if someone had blown out all the lights in their powers of looking and understanding. They were plainly embarrassed by the nude people.

'All sit down,' I said.

We went through the pictures one by one.

'That's a man,' I said. 'He's what you'll be like when you grow up. And breasts are for mums to give babies their milk. Girls will have those when they grow up.'

'My mum has one,' said Susheila, an Indian.

'My cat has 'em,' said Tom.

'Me dog has some in a long line,' said Roody from Barbados. 'She's a girl dog and bitch. She has a lead, but not a bra.'

'My goat has one in Cyprus,' said Turka. 'And my grandmother, she use to put it in my baby mouth when my mum go out and my baby cry.'

They talked about the pictures seriously now. There was no more dead-sounding laughter. They understood something different.

'Well, here are the pictures you've drawn,' I said, but few of them wanted them and those who did just left them lying around.

There was yet more biology to come. Jamaican Sharon tugged my arm. 'I writted a decent word,' she said. 'What my cousin learned me.'

She'd written 'PENIS' in bold red marker pen.

'I can read that,' said Andreas. 'It says PEN IS. You must put somethink else.' He wrote carefully, then showed us the result with a big smile. Now it read 'PEN IS NOT GOOD ONLY PENCIL.'

Occasionally one came across a mother who didn't show animosity only to foreigners but to everyone who didn't conform to her own idea of British standards of normality and 'niceness'.

Such a mum was Mrs Stark, a tall, immaculately turned-out woman, who no one could possibly have guessed lived in substandard housing and had a husband stricken with a terminal disease. Whatever the time of day her two beautiful auburn-haired girls were similarly impeccably dressed. She stood in the playground every morning, holding each daughter tightly by the hand, isolated from all the other children, until the bell went. Any child not of Mrs Stark's choosing who went over to greet her girls was met by her stern injunction, 'Be orf, you garlicky lot!'

One rainy day, Andreas accidentally splashed one of the girls' white socks with the merest speck of water.

'See what you done!' barked Mrs Stark. 'I'm goin' to 'ave you! Rubbish! Animal!'

She might have thumped him if I hadn't intervened. I'd been rounding up the boys who wanted to have the honour of 'being last in school'.

'Well, we're all animals, you know,' I said. 'The only difference is that some are old, others young, some big, some little. A clever woman and a good mum like you should know that.'

'Them Greek kids,' she muttered confidentially, 'I could clout 'em. We try to keep out of the way but they still come after us.'

'They're probably attracted by your nice clothes,' I told her. 'Anyway, don't try to clout Andreas – his dad might clout you back.'

She went off into the cloakroom where she wandered around and around, changing and choosing pegs until she was certain that her daughters' coats would hang hygienically next to the belongings of a nice, clean, native, Anglo-Saxon child.

But not long afterwards we found that one of the coats lay soaking wet in the sink. I had my suspicions even while I asked the class, 'Who put a coat in the water today?'

Andreas smiled. 'It fell in and I never took it out.' We wrote a letter apologising to Mrs Stark but, apart from glaring at me, she said nothing. Hers was mainly a smouldering animosity.

The children were no angels. As I've said, a fair description would be lovable devils. But most of them did own up, whatever the crime.

I shall never forget the look of astonishment on the face of one of the teachers, Pera Bennum, when she walked into the office one day. Pera was a white South African who had suffered grievously in her own country for her strongly held anti-Apartheid views. Now she cared lovingly for children of many colours and many nations. An elegant woman, she had a toughness of spirit that belied a seemingly fragile charm. She was to become a dear friend.

At this time, however, she was bewildered, caught between justified irritation and her own sharp sense of fun. And as ever, at such moments, her South African accent showed through.

'Those kids,' she said, 'they've tricked me – completely! They pinched my money and then gave it back to me to mind for them.'

She explained, 'They've always given me money to mind and I've always made a list and beside each name put the correct amount. This afternoon when they asked for their money back I doled it out to them – the correct amount to each – and they were most polite. "Thanks, Miss Bennum," they said, just like parrots. I felt so pleased about them saying thanks so nicely. Then, later, when I looked into my purse, it was empty! I'd been tricked!'

We both sat there stunned for a minute and then fell about laughing.

'What did they say when you charged them with it?' I asked.

'Oh, they were honest about that. They said, "Well, you're our mum, ain't you? Can't we take your money?" Almost as if I ought to be flattered. The funny thing was that I did feel flattered in a way.'

'Well, we're not going to have this sort of thing going on!' I said firmly.

I decided on a banking experiment and tried it out on my own class. I bought a money-box and told the children they could put their money in it but only take out exactly what they'd contributed. The children helped to run the bank. Tina was put in charge of the accounts. She was not only popular but also extremely strong.

Later our financial efforts were dedicated to bolstering up the school fund. It wasn't unusual for parents to knock at my door and say, 'Here's a few bob for the box.' When funds got low I'd ask children to sing a song. Those who said they'd rather not paid a forfeit. Almost invariably, the Greek boys, for some reason which I never understood, preferred to pay, although they sang heartily when they sang together.

It was all done good-humouredly and loyally but then, that was the kind of school it was. Children and parents alike were fiercely loyal to this school. It was an open place, where children could talk from the heart about their joys and sadnesses. Teachers were 'family'. In fact, the loyalty these children had given to their villages and families in their own lands was now freely given to the school.

As for us teachers, we gave them all, children and parents, our utter respect. We tried to learn the names of all children and all the parents, and make use of this knowledge. In some cases names were all they really had. Names were not only their identity but also their dignity.

So when at last the news came in 1969 of my appointment as Headmistress of another multiracial school I could only greet it with mixed feelings, although it had been the Headmistress of my present school who had made me feel that I was now ready to assume the extra responsibilities.

It was a day, in fact, of both sadness and fulfilment. The school had been an inspiration for what I might hope to achieve in the future but the future was, of course, unknown. I was leaving teachers who *accepted* the rights of children and spent an enormous amount of time helping them towards a feeling of responsibility. I was leaving a hard-won environment where there was order, consideration, personal contribution and always the spirit of give and take.

Beryl with her class as Deputy Head of Montem School, 1968

Teaching at this school had been to work with love, so, for a moment, I felt empty and dark inside – but only for a moment. Looking at my own class, a feeling of intense satisfaction came over me. It was as if I'd shared a very special loaf with these children.

'Will you come and see us, Miss Gilroy?' asked Sharon. She'd been the one who'd cried when I first took over. She'd felt cheated. She was the first black child who'd ever really rejected me. She wanted a nice white teacher – the same as her sister had. She painted her hands with white paint to mask her blackness. She only stopped this practice when her mother clipped her smartly on the top of her head with her umbrella. But now she wanted to be like me. What was more, she wanted to be a teacher.

The staff gave me a farewell party. I left it late but some of my class were still waiting in a tight group to wave me on.

'Goodbye, Miss Gilroy,' they called. 'Goodbye – you did like us, didn't you? We like everybody in the world.'

I could only nod, look away and run for my bus.

13

'Someone's happy'

So three weeks later, I came to my present school. I had been short-listed for three schools and had chosen to be interviewed for this one. I had been regarded as a non-starter, as the schools in this part of London appealed, I had been told, to the teaching elite. A week before, a colleague had warned, 'You'll never get that. There'll be several Heads going up for the job.' I was fairly relaxed about the interview, however. I faced a formidable panel, who asked pertinent questions which called for informed answers. I loved children and now I was confident that I had the ability to be a Headteacher, with its administrative responsibilities, despite my love of the classroom and the day-to-day contact with a specific set of children.

At first meeting my school seemed to me like some monstrous animal with a cacophonous voice and syncopated pulse. Dazed, I stood in the hall while children surged through it in a kind of happy fury of personal indulgence. One tall, heavy youngster, using his hands like a swimmer doing the breast-stroke, swept little ones out of his way. And parents, it seemed to me, stuck out like leading actors in all this hubbub. The children were the swarming, 'rhubarb'-ing extras, doing their own thing.

Oh, they were 'free' all right. Freely responding and reacting at random, freely ignoring other people, freely rushing from happening to happening with whoops and yells and delirious abandon. But never 'free' in the true sense of the word. This was licence.

I doubted whether I'd ever seen so much disintegrated energy. 'If I'm going to survive here,' I thought, 'this has to become different – and the sooner the better.'

During those early days I could make little sense of the attitudes around me. My responsibility, as far as I could see it, didn't extend to defending such a hit-or-miss philosophy, or accepting its resulting hurly-burly.

Good infant teaching needs no labels. It is a positive, productive interaction between all the children and the environment, and the teacher is the experienced partner in this learning situation. He or she isn't infallible or omnipotent, but should be capable of striking all the chords of potential. This must be the way ahead.

But first it had to be realised that I hadn't been made Headteacher as part of the rumoured policy of the Inner London Education Authority – a policy called 'kindness to blacks'. After this fact was accepted, I was able to put into practice my own beliefs, rooted in knowledge and experience.

I decided to make the daily assemblies an integral part of school life so that I could touch children as they'd never been touched before. I began by letting the children feel that it was a time that belonged to them – a time to share their experiences. Assembly was no longer a routine, formalised affair. In some ways it became an infants' forum. Often I would tell a story – perhaps about some legendary child – and the children would take part in the ensuing discussion and sometimes continue it in their own classrooms.

Beryl leading assembly as Headteacher of Beckford School
in West Hampstead, London, 1973

I would join them at play in the playground. I explained
to them that my own room was also part of school and it was
a place where they were welcome to discuss anything with
me. I had special little chairs and tables put there for this
purpose.

School work was to be based on the group methods I'd first
experimented with at Bob's school. It is known in the textbooks as 'group dynamics', but it's really a way in which a child
can contribute to a common topic or project.

A child chooses a friend, perhaps two, or perhaps even a
competitor, but once the choice is made, the group is formed
and can only be altered after each activity. The groups are now
committed to carrying out a task that is academic only in the
sense that anything can be truly academic for infants.

The group know the rules and they themselves must apply the rules. They accept that the task must be completed, and that *they* must assess it and sign their names to it.

Children of that age can assess. Their assessments, in fact, can often be devastating, and their candour fascinating. They must judge what they've done and take pride in it.

This wasn't – and still isn't – the normal type of multiracial school. A complicating factor, due to the circumstances of its catchment area, was its very strong middle-class element. It was soon obvious to me that this must have some interesting effects and on reflection it is that all the working-class children want to be middle class. If a little black child has any particular aspiration, it's to be a middle-class white. Up to the age of seven, given a choice that's what they'll choose.

At times I can't help feeling a little sad that they give up their indigenous cultures in this way. The copying of mannerisms can also be slavish and a trifle absurd. Some copy even the sticking out little fingers when they drink their milk.

The parents also absorbed middle-class attitudes. Since middle-class parents were mainly articulate and keen on getting the best for their children, it wasn't long before *all* parents were reacting in the same way – talking of their rights and putting their views, however ill-formed they might be. Some parents talked of their responsibilities and this was good. This was the truly encouraging part of it. They were expressing both their expectations for the children and their willingness to help the children achieve them.

All this was to pay dividends when eventually we appointed a reading co-ordinator, who was expected to advise parents and children about kinds and levels of reading material. She arranged book displays, contacted book clubs and worked closely with a local children's librarian.

I knew from the start that at this school I had to build a sense of growth and achievement. I had little time for pique or paranoia. My prime job was to help each child to know me personally as a considerate, sympathetic friend.

And the children, as always, talked freely to me . . .

The black children, again as always, had their very special problems – many due to fostering experiences in early childhood.

'I was white once,' said Roger, who had been fostered by white middle-class parents in Brighton. 'I got black when I came home.'

Tunde, from Nigeria, kept referring to his father as 'The Man' or 'That Black Man'. He just couldn't relate to black people. He even disowned his own photograph. And when I persuaded him to paint his self-portrait and colour it, he wailed, 'Stop it! I don't want all that blackness on me.'

Many immigrant children looked upon Englishness as some sort of virtue. I suggested to their parents that they ought to give their children some insight into the culture from which they came. But some were too tired to bother, after working all day, and others didn't know how to start. Some regarded a child's self-concept as of no importance whatsoever. They were here to get qualifications to build a future, and to make a better life. That was all there was to it.

This idea of wiping out a complete background saddened me. I told the children about my own girlhood in the village by the sea where I'd grown up. I told them about Anansi, the Spider Man, who is our equivalent of Brer Rabbit. I told them too of West Indian festivals, birthdays and weddings. I taught them songs and ring-games and, when I danced them, they tittered at first but then joined in.

The West Indian children seemed so ashamed of any music or, indeed, anything that was black or African. I suppose they felt they got no support from such things. Once I gave them a picture showing a group of people and asked them to pick the bad people. The black children picked out all the blacks. The people they picked were well dressed and smiling but it made no difference. 'They look like bad people,' the black children said.

Kings, queens, angels and fairies for ever presented a problem. They just couldn't be black until we decided they should. Once I showed a poster of an old black woman surrounded by fruits and flowers. She wore a scarf on her head and her face was deeply lined with the dignity of hard work. Some black children laughed nervously and some looked away and covered their eyes. Those who didn't criticised her. 'I don't like her face,' said Sam, a Ghanaian. 'She looks like a monkey. She's too black. But I like inside her hands. That's white.'

Some of the children expressed dislike of the mannerisms of their parents, the sound of native-talk, the smell of their food and their whole lifestyle.

Black parents had their problems, too. Often it was rejection by children who had been returned to them at school age after being fostered for years.

'My father is dead,' said Willie. 'He died when a van broke his heart. He was cleaning the engine. It came down and broke his heart.'

But the next day I saw his father in the flesh. 'You're supposed to be dead,' I told him.

He laughed ruefully. 'Willie tells everybody say I dead. He hate me since the day we had a botheration at home. If I dead he will go back to the people who grow him up.'

'What's the problem?' I asked.

'It's the work I do – no dignity in it. No future. You have talk they hand you your cards. Yet I have to do the work. I hate myself. I run home and hate my family.'

Adetola, a pretty little Nigerian, came to school each morning in tears. I could see that she had been smacked. I discovered that she never spoke to her parents – whatever they did, whatever they asked her. She would speak to us, and laugh and joke, once her early-morning tears had subsided. But should her parents appear on the scene she would relapse into pouting and sulking.

'The people she was with prepare her some bad habits,' her mother explained to me. 'I give her food. She hold her nose then she eat it like it will make her choke on it. She is my child but I wish she was not my child.'

Sometimes it seemed to me that I spent half my working life trying to achieve reconciliation between children and parents . . .

Then there was the kind of child who came to us utterly confused by incidents in his background. Michael, a three-year-old Greek boy, had been looked after in all by about a dozen childminders. He was listless, greedy and unable to play. When he did break out of his lethargy he wreaked havoc everywhere. His grandmother, patiently coached by the nursery teacher, tried to cope and slowly he began to change. He smiled. He talked. He shared.

But one day I saw him with another child, even younger

than himself, coming out of a sweetshop with handfuls of sweets.

'Where did you get the money?' I asked.

'From my granny's purse,' he said. 'She's sleeping in the chair.'

I followed the children home and was met by Michael's mother on the doorstep, wringing her hands and wailing in her own language. Inside, Granny lay dead in her rocking chair.

From that day onwards, whenever he was upset or thwarted, Michael pretended to be dead.

Chaka, a black African, was one of the most difficult children I ever met. Cruel and aggressive beyond belief, he was the terror of the playground and the children nicknamed him Godzilla, the monster who fights King Kong. He was delighted with the name until he found out what it meant and then he thumped them all into the ground.

Chaka's trouble was the rigorous treatment he received at home. This was made all too apparent when his parents, who had refused all our efforts to get psychological help for him, at last arrived to discuss him.

The father, a highly educated man, gave us a demonstration of how to deal with his son. Seizing his ears in both hands he first scolded him in his own language and then thumped him soundly.

Next he asked me for a piece of paper and proceeded to give me written permission to perform on Chaka in exactly the same way.

'Beating is the traditional method of punishment for our people,' he explained to me patiently. 'Beating is like tying the twig. With beating it will not incline. It will grow straight.'

One thing was clear. Chaka was so mortally afraid of his parents that if ever I needed to straighten the twig I had only to take up the phone and pretend to call his ever-loving daddy. At once Chaka changed miraculously from a raving lion into a gentle lamb.

Then quite suddenly there was the threat of a teachers' strike, of day-to-day disruptiveness. The children were excited about it. Some urged me to strike, close the school and 'support the workers'. 'I will,' I said, 'provided you can do two things. First you must get your parents and the two teachers who want me to support an unofficial strike to convince me that all the children of working mothers would be taken care of for as long as the strike lasts. And next you must show me that all the rights of action and opinion are on your side.'

'What does that mean?' said Aeron.

'Damn it,' said John. 'It means why have we got all the rights, and who's going to mind the children.'

They left my room arguing among themselves. As I ate my lunch there was a tap on my open door. A poker-faced parent came in. 'Paul's teacher is going on strike,' she said, 'and you aren't going to black-leg his class. You're like my husband – always on the fence.'

'You're forgetting one thing,' I said. 'My leg's already black.' She looked at me as if she'd like to make sure.

'Why are you such a stirrer?' I added gently. 'Don't you have any tender moments in your life? Go home and hold your husband's hand. Then go walk on the grass – barefoot.' She looked at me as if I had suddenly gone out of my mind. Then she went off chuckling at the nonsense I'd told her. Children's dislikes are pretty short-lived but at that time strikes and the fire-bell were top of the charts. The fire-bell was a mechanical noise to which they were unused and they found it strange and frightening.

They told me some stories about strikes.

'I had to give myself lunch. My key fell in the stew. I couldn't get it out. I burnt myself and I cried all on my own.'

'A man opened his van door and told me to get in. I ran up the allotments and hid in someone's garden. I heard him looking for me.'

'I put my coat on the heater. It smelt funny. The landlord came down and put us out in the rain. He didn't want us to start a fire.'

'When it's a strike and my mummy stays home, she's nasty a lot of times. Then she rows with my daddy and they both have no money. Then they pick on me and say, "Where does she learn her habits from?"'

'My brothers they did eat all the cornflakes and my mum didn't have no money to buy food and me mum said, "We is West Indians. People expect us to beg for money so we ain't going to beg for none. We goin' act like we is decent people."'

I had to defend my position time after time. I was even told that more support for the workers would be forthcoming from a white Head.

'Yes,' I agreed. 'One who shares the same ideas as they do.'

When it came to choosing between the children and the decrees of some remote body who didn't know the problems the children would have to face, I chose the children.

Years before, I was given a taste of the attitude of the union to people like me. I applied for a clerical job with one of the leading unions in this country. They rejected me on colour. The

Communist among them was so embarrassed, he came round to my digs to apologise for the behaviour of those gentlemen who interviewed me.

The proliferation of Asian children seemed, oddly enough, to heighten their problems within the school. Certainly it seemed harder for them to mix with the rest of the school. They would hang together, prattle away in their several languages, and defy any intrusions by what seemed to the English despicable methods. They wouldn't use their fists – perhaps they didn't know how. But they would pinch, tweak noses and ears, bend fingers and pull hair. It wasn't playing the game – not by any English standards.

Even the parents, rather self-consciously, felt they had to draw my attention to this and I explained that children from within an enclosed foreign culture called upon it in many subtle and varied ways.

Some of the children continued to be unhappy about their obvious points of difference. One morning, Yasmina, from Somaliland, walked into my office in a most tearful state. Was it that old bogey 'hair' again? Black children were most hair-conscious. Hair-braiding, for instance, provoked taunts from other children of 'You got snakes in your hair'.

Yasmina's sorrows had a different source. 'Miss Gilroy,' she sobbed, 'Sophie says I am oily in my hair and spicy in my smell. And she won't play with me.'

'Look, darling,' I said, 'your hair does have oil and you do smell of saffron. I like it.'

We went off to assembly hand in hand.

'Can anyone guess the name of Yasmina's smell?' I asked later.

'Disinfectant,' said Hungarian Tim.

'No, teak oil,' said John, our knowledgeable grandson of a lord.

'You're both wrong,' I said, 'it's saffron. You're rather backward about your smells, aren't you? You ought to have a "Smell Table" in your class and then you could smell nice things like garlic, incense, boot polish, curry powder and toilet soap.'

This got the children talking about aspects of cultures they liked, and subsequently, when we mounted a Human Studies programme, we tried to include music, religion and food.

We invited a band of African musicians to play for us, and, led by a pudgy extrovert in native garb, the group sang and danced to ear-splitting music. The next day some of the children offered to sing their national anthems but, oddly enough, there were no offers from the English. They only seemed to recognise 'God Save the Queen' after considerable prompting. The most militant among them protested!

'We don't sing that,' said Jenny, the little daughter of middle-class intellectuals. 'We hate the Queen.'

'Yes, we do,' John chipped in. 'She has too many houses. She should give them to Shelter.'

'Oh, come on now,' I said. 'Someone's been giving you a line. You must know the national anthem, mustn't you, if you're going to hate it really well. It comes under General Knowledge.'

'It's a nonsense rhyme,' insisted Jenny. 'My mother told me.'

'Anyway, we're all going to start learning it now,' I said. 'Nonsense rhymes are good for the soul.'

We repeated the words and sang the tune again and again.

'Now sing yourselves to sleep with it tonight,' I suggested, and they smiled their happy seven-year-old smiles.

Beryl in the library at Beckford School, 1970

But I was to hear more about the National Anthem – more, of course, in controversial terms. When we sang it at one of our functions, a parent who was usually friendly and most helpful got up in the middle of it, walked out, and only returned when we'd finished. I was furious. He started to explain but I cut in,

'I don't care how much you hate the Queen and I don't care what you stand for. All I'm concerned with is the example of good manners, self-control and tolerance you set here in this school.'

Tolerance did take root but at times there were relapses.

Gregory was so conditioned by his rigid religious background to be definite about the things he should hate that a skullcap sparked off his anti-Semitism and he declared, on seeing a picture of the Pope, 'What's this bloody Jew doing here wearing his skullcap?'

Rama, a nice but now very worried little Indian boy, complained that a white child had told him to 'f—— off'.

'Perhaps he doesn't know any really nice words,' I consoled him. It was probably true in this particular case.

'He doesn't,' said the astonishingly articulate Mark, 'or he could so easily say "sexual intercourse", couldn't he?'

Still 'broadening out', still seeking tolerance, we bought a skeleton, as a kind of lowest and inevitable common denominator of us all. I used to ask the children to guess its race and was amused by the way in which some of them used it to flatter me.

'He's obviously a coloured man,' said Joseph, an Israeli, 'because he looks so intelligent.'

Many parents, at first, couldn't understand our attitude – found it hard to accept our system of working.

I remember the German parent who bemoaned his seven-year-old's apparent lack of commitment to school. He was certain, he said, that his son would develop into 'an English *laissez-faire* worker who would quarrel over differentials he didn't deserve'.

What it all amounted to was that, whatever part of the world they came from, parents initially, at least, yearned for the education system they'd left behind. The French, West Indians and Greeks wanted to see their children handcuffed to their tasks. The Asians would have liked passive children chanting their lessons – preferably under palms. The Italian and Spanish mums thought school a kind of conspiracy to deprive them of their right to mother their children and in doing so occupy their own time at home.

From the English there was a more subtle and varied reaction, as one would expect. The variations stretched from 'you're doing a jolly good job' to regarding us as highly paid childminders. Many had 'read a book' and knew all about teaching.

Parents, of course, were often under discussion when I held my staff-training sessions. I used to insist that the parents should never be measured against ourselves, as teachers, our own parents, or even our own ideas of the good parent. In their own eyes, the mothers and fathers who brought their children to our school were good parents – providing food and clothes, shelter and support. I do believe, however, that no matter how hard teachers may try, some black parents will always suspect a teacher's motives. This is the consequence of years of subservience and paternalism.

'How can whites ever understand our hopes, our aspirations, our feelings and all the sources of our resentment? How can they possibly do this from within their mother-of-pearl shells?' This sums up what black parents ask me.

For my own part, most black parents said they were happy that I'd come to the school. They gave, and have given me, their trust, their love and respect. Only a few have tended to think that because I was a black who 'had made it', I must have outgrown or forgotten their problems.

The school was still one of factions and status groups but we inched forward, always seeking our own highly individual integration. One important stepping-stone was a May festival with the theme of Woodland Folk. The whole problem of costumes and props I dropped firmly into the laps of parents. They knew what we wanted and how they could help. We had to summon Robin Hood and his Merry Men and a whole host of nymphs, fairies, elves, gnomes, birds, bees, butterflies and other creatures out of winter quarters, to greet the Queen of the May. The parents grappled with the task with daunting resolution. Participation became the very air breathed.

When the great day came, we were all resolutely English despite the fact that the Queen of the May was a Russian child all dressed in white, and carrying red carnations, and that the boys and girls who danced round the Maypole were of so many different colours. The pride of parents in what their children were doing – in what they themselves had done – knew no bounds. It is a pride that has gone on growing over the years. Parents came to realise that the invitation lay open to them to become partners in the education of their children, and they accepted it.

And so, after all the early tumult and confusion, we settled down and school became more and more a place where children played and worked in harmony and contentment; where we never lost sight of that all-important trinity – staff, parents and children all working together for a common end – not merely a school but a community. And that's what we are today.

Once a week parents are invited to attend class assemblies taken by the children, who show the work that's being done and the interests that are being pursued in the classroom. The teachers talk to parents who accept that education involves and includes them. Parents, when it is their turn, take the assemblies and tell us about their work and their interests. All nationalities of parents take part. We have had rope tricks from an Indian parent who ran away to join a circus when he was a boy, and well-known television actors among the parents have told us about the programmes in which they appear. I expect parents to attend our functions and unashamedly encourage the children to insist that they do.

Beryl in the playground at Beckford School, 1971

In our Parent–Teacher Association and in our parents' classes we discuss aspects of child development and produce our own infant school magazine, as well as information about our aims and purposes for parents who are considering sending their children to our school. We admit to being ignorant about some things, or tired, or happy, or sad, and parents accept that in matters which concern a child we like if possible to include the child in all the discussions. From time to time we teachers discuss school rules with the children and help them to recognise those which we have made for ourselves and those which truly affect them. I point out to the parents that it is perfectly normal for them to love their children and yet not like them at all because parents need to be reassured that there are no feelings about their children which are decreed by nature. I help the staff to see that children are people – some nice, some nasty, but the nastiness the child has acquired hasn't necessarily, as some people would like to think, come from Mum, Dad or even the teacher.

There are days that linger in my mind not only because they are marked by some incident but also because they show the direction we've taken. I remember such a day in the summer of 1970.

It began well when Ester came in to see me. Ester was the little German girl I'd admitted to the school on the day when Sue had arrived so unexpectedly to set me raking over the coals of my time with Mr Coppett and Co. Ester hadn't possessed a single word of English that first morning but now, triumphantly, she read me a whole page from her reading book – in tones of purest Hampstead.

Furthermore, she added, as a kind of bonus, that another little girl was performing a strip-tease of sorts in the playground at that very instant. I find, as a teacher, that dull moments are always a rarity.

'Someone's happy'

It was a day when we had the windows open to let in the summer air and so the sound of children was all about me. It's hard for me to concentrate in such circumstances for I'm always curious about what the children are actually saying. Often, in this way, I glean treasures for my diary.

The afternoon found me looking out of my window with special interest at the wooden shed that stood in the playground. Already there was a lively gaggle of mothers in it. Mums were using it more and more as a sort of meeting place. We were already some way advanced in giving this school its second identity – that of a community school.

It was while I was wondering how we could further use the shed that my secretary told me I had a visitor. It was my friend, Pera Bennum, from my last school.

I was delighted to see her after so many months but I couldn't help noticing that she looked thinner and that, in spite of her usual air of quiet elegance, some of the sparkle was missing.

'I've had a minor op,' she said, 'but now I'm raring to go. If I don't start work again soon I'll begin to think I've really got something wrong with me.'

The words were indeed prophetic. She'd come to seek part-time work and soon she was to join us. But in far too short a time she left us for ever – one of the most brilliant teachers I'd ever come across and one of the finest human beings.

But that afternoon, it was a time for reunion, for chuckling over the past, for musing about the future. There was plenty to chuckle about, in shared past experience. How had the incorrigibles fared after I'd left? I asked about one in particular.

Pera laughed as we recalled a boy whose doting auntie was

'on the game'. Auntie had bought her cherub a tape recorder for his birthday – but what had cherub done with it? Put it under her bed, switched it on, then brought the recording to school.

Yes, the incorrigibles were still incorrigible. It was reassuring in its perverse way.

How about the old Greek grandmother who had hovered over the playground like a hooded black eagle, waiting to snatch up her little granddaughter away from all peril of alien boys? We'd experimented by channelling her maternal instincts into the school nursery. Yes, said Pera, she was still there, the squarest peg in the roundest of holes.

It was when we stopped looking backwards, when our thoughts went forward, that I found myself concentrating with a clarity that could only be due to Pera's presence. Pera had, on occasions, at our last school talked to her class in simple terms about the United Nations Charter and the Declaration of Human Rights. Now, as we chatted about the form and aims of a multiracial school, it was almost as if I were making my own Declaration of what such a school should be.

Perhaps I was just thinking aloud, clearing my own mind.

I said that if I had to colour the school I would like to have, I would use the rain-washed greens of early spring and the lively yellows of summer. It would be a school where we would be concerned with the present lives of the children and yet always consider sources from the past. A place where we would lead the children towards adventure and experience, where thought and feeling would work in harmony and where the children's dues would be kindness, courtesy and loving justice. The environment would be alive but not overstimulating. The fare that was offered would be neither stale nor underdone.

Always we would realise, as teachers, that we ourselves were aggressive or complacent, or arrogant, and when we came up against these same qualities in children or parents we would recognise them and react with as much compassion as if we were dealing with our own families.

We would speak to the children, I thought, in a living way, not in the age-old 'special' teacher's voice, or in the jargon of status. We would work with the children as an artist works – patiently, yet potently. Children would question us, unafraid, and by helping them to understand our purposes we would understand them better ourselves. The ultimate aim would be to bring the children to the point where they would face up to themselves and their true feelings.

All this was the text for our long talk that afternoon. All this and much besides.

Pera, since she was to join me, wanted to know about the additional element in my school – the middle-class children and their parents.

'What of the really clever parents?' she asked.

'Well, they vary,' I said, 'but few ever say, like working-class parents, "children can't all be clever". They find it difficult to accept the not-so-clever. And the children, of course, do tend to look upon us as not as clever as their parents. It's done by a sort of subtle deprecation. "My mummy really is rather clever" – are you?'

As we spoke young Ned popped his head in, to make a middle-class point.

He'd just returned from a year in America.

'Welcome back, Ned,' I said. 'What did you miss most?'

He thought about it for a moment, and then said, 'The class

system, I think, really. The people next door to us out there had absolutely masses of money – but, oh, they were so vulgar. When they came into our house they'd say, "Well, wha dya know!" almost every time we spoke.'

'Oh, yes?' I said. 'What else?'

'The school was most odd, too. The first day they fought with me. But after that I plucked up my courage and kicked a few shins.'

'Rather un-English, wasn't it?' I said.

'But very American – I can tell you,' he replied.

Pera was stunned. 'Have you got any more like that?' she asked, after he'd gone.

'Yes, quite a few in each of the top three classes,' I said. Our talk that afternoon was rippled by several of these little interruptions. The children flitted to and fro as they always do. Once I left the room to an urgent 'Please, will you put the fairground music on?' The children loved having their favourite records played during break.

But, at last, it was time for her to go and so I walked her downstairs, and then because it had been so nice to see her again I walked all the way with her.

When I got back it was playtime and there waiting for me was the Deputy Head with that look on her face that presaged an awkward situation. I read it at once, even before she could put it into words, because I'd read it before.

'Two people to see you,' she announced in tones of foreboding. 'A mother and a grandmother. The old woman has been saying the most awful things about black people. Would you like me to try and handle her?'

I shook my head. 'Thanks, but no. I've been insulted by the

real experts. She won't last longer than they did.'

The two women sat tense and unsmiling outside the door.

'Good day,' I said, offering my hand.

The younger one took it – but the older one wouldn't. She muttered under her breath and stared her hate at me out of rock-hard blue eyes. She folded her arms tightly across her chest.

'You're Gregory's mother,' I said to the younger woman. 'And this lady?'

'She's my mum.'

'You know we've had rather a lot of trouble with Gregory lately?' I said. 'So I felt I had to write and tell you.'

'That's why we come,' said Grandma.

I told them that Gregory had been bullying the younger children and suggested they might help me to curb his violence.

'You're not going to tell us what to bloody do,' said Grandma.

'You know what?' she added. 'You know where you ought to be? You ought to be on telly with them Brooke Bond tea chimps. That's where you ought to bloody be – not here, telling us.'

'Those chimps have got their work to do,' I said to her, 'and I've got mine. Part of it happens to be talking to parents. Come on, now!' I joked, although I'd never felt less like it. 'It's high time you moved from the disreputable to the respectable. That means being a nice old lady, doesn't it?'

'Yes, Mum,' said the daughter, 'now you shut up, Mum.'

But the old woman still dribbled her insults. 'Bleedin' blacks – gettin' above their station . . .'

When they'd gone, after my uneasy peace-offering of a cup of coffee, I held my head for a while. It throbbed with the pressure of it all. Perhaps after my high-minded session with Pera it had been ordained to restore the balance. But it was still dispiriting, to say the least.

As I walked upstairs, however, I heard a child singing. It was Terry. Funny! I'd never heard him singing on his own before. I caught up with him in the corridor – a seven-year-old with a tooth-gappy grin.

'Someone's happy,' I said. 'You like school or something?'

He nodded briskly.

'What's so nice about it, then?' I asked, thinking in terms of our new library books and equipment, and my eager new young staff.

He looked at me for quite a while and then turned on the fullness of his gappy smile.

'You!' he said, suddenly, explosively, and then he was off and away.

That truly helped. That really made my day.

Timeline

Dr Beryl Gilroy, BSc, MA Ed, PhD

30 August 1924	Beryl Agatha Answick is born in Berbice, British Guiana
1943–5	Teacher's Diploma (First Class), Government Training College, Georgetown, British Guiana
1946–51	Lecturer, Urban School, British Guiana Lecturer, UNICEF Food Programme for the Disadvantaged, British Guiana
1952–3	Advanced Diploma, Child Development, University of London
1954	Classroom Teacher, St Joseph in the Fields, Bethnal Green, London
1955	Classroom Teacher, Bell Street School, Lisson Grove, London
1956	Classroom Teacher, London County Council
1960–2	Froebel Teacher's Diploma, Froebel Educational Institute, London
1959–62	BSc in Psychology, University of London
1963–5	Diploma in English as a Second Language, University of London
1965–8	Part-time Classroom Teacher, Tufnell Park Primary School, London
1968–9	Deputy Headteacher, Montem Primary School, London

1968–74	Race Relations Board, North West London Committee
1969–82	Headteacher, Beckford Primary School, London
1974	Visiting Lecturer, Pepperdine University, California
1976	*Black Teacher* is first published
1975–7	Pre-MA course, Psychology of Adolescence, University of London
1979–2001	Founder member, Camden Black Sisters
1980	MA in Education (Distinction), Sussex University
1980–3	Counsellor and Psychotherapist, Tavistock Clinic, London
1982	*In For a Penny* wins Greater London Council Creative Writing Ethnic Minorities Prize
1983–9	Educational Consultant/Researcher, Centre for Multicultural Education at the Institute of Education, University of London
1983–7	PhD in Counselling Psychology, Century University, USA
1985	*Frangipani House* wins Greater London Council Creative Writing Prize
1992	*Stedman and Joanna* wins the Guyana Literary Prize
1994	Clothes displayed in the Victoria and Albert Museum exhibition 'Street Style: From Sidewalk to Catwalk', and acquired for the permanent collections
1995	Honorary Doctorate, University of North London
1996	Honoured by the Association of Caribbean Women Writers and Scholars

Timeline

2000   Honorary Fellowship, Institute of Education,
University of London

4 April 2001   Passes away at the Royal Free Hospital, London

2004   Clothes displayed in the Victoria and Albert
Museum exhibition 'Black British Style'

Beryl receiving her Honorary Fellowship at the Institute
of Education, London, 2000

Publications

Educational Series and Companion Guides

Blue Water Readers, three titles (London: Longmans, 1961)
Blue Water Readers Teacher's Guide: A Handbook on the Teaching of Reading (London: Longmans, 1961)
The Green and Gold Readers for Guyana, four titles (Trinidad: Longmans, 1967–71)
Nippers and *Little Nippers*, thirteen titles (Macmillan, 1970–5)
Yellow Bird Readers, three titles (London: Macmillan, 1974–8)

Children's Fiction

Carnival of Dreams (Oxford: Macmillan, 1980)
In For a Penny (Oxford: Cassell, 1980)

Memoir

Black Teacher (London: Cassell, 1976; repr. Bogle-L'Ouverture, 1994; repr. Faber, 2021)
Sunlight on Sweet Water (Leeds: Peepal Tree, 1994)

Fiction

Frangipani House (London: Heinemann, 1986)
Boy-Sandwich (Heinemann International, 1989)
Stedman and Joanna (New York: Vantage, 1991)
Gather the Faces (Leeds: Peepal Tree, 1996)
In Praise of Love and Children (Leeds: Peepal Tree, 1996)
Inkle and Yarico (Leeds: Peepal Tree, 1996)
The Green Grass Tango (Leeds: Peepal Tree, 2001)

Essays and Poetry

Leaves in the Wind: Collected Writings (London: Mango, 1998)
Echoes and Voices (New York: Vantage, 1991)